Bankruptcy And Survival In Times Of Economic Uncertainty

Bankruptcy And Survival In Times Of Economic Uncertainty

Practical Tips for Surviving the Economic Downturn/Recession

Shafii A. Ndanusa MBA, ACCA

This book was printed in the United States of America.

To order additional copies of this book, contact:
Xlibris Corporation
0-800-644-6988
www.XlibrisPublishing.co.uk
Orders@XlibrisPublishing.co.uk
302908

CONTENTS

PART THREE

CRAFTING THE ECONOMIC SURVIVAL PLAN

DEDICATION

To the millions of people who are victims of the present
modern economic systems . . . in all nations of the world

ACKNOWLEDGMENTS

A special learning experience comes with writing books. You come to learn that every successful effort that results in a book is in fact the result of team effort. So while the author of a book takes final credit for its creation, the real credit is actually for those that made tremendous contributions in the process of completing the book.

The biggest support I received came from members of my family. I must thank them especially for their never ending words of encouragement.

Because this book has a slight touch of academic flavor to it, I would also like to thank my academic tutors at the university who made sure I was sufficiently drilled in the areas of business and economic research. Some of my greatest lessons were learnt from fellow students and colleagues at work. As I recall each of those lessons, I wish to thank all those who have contributed to this effort knowingly or unknowingly.

INTRODUCTION

I am quite certain that a lot of people will agree with me that some of the most disturbing pictures they have ever laid eyes on are those of starving children in the Horn of Africa. This part of the world, notorious for its harsh climatic conditions as well as seemingly unending human strife is by far one of the most difficult parts of the world to thrive in, in economic terms. The pictures of some people wallowing in abject poverty, starvation, disease, destitution and death from this region of the world is almost unbearable for most people. For me, each day I set eyes on even one of those images I find it difficult to eat for the rest of the day. I don't know what it is like for other people but the experience ranges from a feeling of pity for the victims, personal sadness and disappointment with governments and political leadership.

If you carefully take a look at the experiences of the victims of the Great Depressions of the 1930's in the United of America, you will notice a similar pattern. When the drought hit the region and compounded the already fragile economic situation, farmers who are normally shielded to a certain extent from an economic recession became completely exposed to the economic crisis. A lot of small farmers were out of business. Families lost not only their farms, savings and other investments, they also lost their homes. Joblessness and homelessness practically turned individuals and households into destitute situations. Large numbers of people lived on hand-outs, fed from the refuse bins and roamed the country in search of a better life. The crime rate soared in most American cities in addition to the high incidence of poor mental health.

The difference between the Horn of Africa scenario that is being experienced now and the experience of the victims of the Great Depression of the 1930's in the United States is simply time and location. People, all over the world are concerned about providing first for their physiological needs of basic food, basic clothing, basic shelter and basic health. When the provision of these needs are threatened either by natural or man-made factors, the very survival of the individual itself is at risk. This threat creates anxiety and leads to desperation. The resulting consequence is of course conflict and instability within the political and economic environment.

With the looming European sovereign debt crisis, the International Monetary Fund is indeed of the view that the global economy is approaching a 'dangerous new phase'. The way the collapse of the housing market in the United States triggered a financial crisis in the United States and thus led to the global financial crisis of 2007/2008 is still fresh in the memories of most victims. The contagion effect of the collapse of a major industry in a major world economic powerhouse cannot be over emphasized.

The question that is being asked repeatedly is that who will bail out a nation that has become bankrupt. While the experience of a national bankruptcy is not new to the world, what appears to be new is indeed the phase of the experience. This phase includes many industrialized European nations that have been traditionally regarded as having been successful. These nations characterized by high level of economic integration and interdependence with other major economic players pose a threat not only to themselves but the entire euro zone and indeed the global economy.

When the global financial industry was threatened in the 2007/2008 global financial crisis, national governments generally responded with fiscal stimulus packages and huge bank bailouts. Now that the crisis has been amplified from the financial industry to the entire domestic economies of some European countries, who and when will these nations be bailed out? And will the provided solutions be a long term solution or another cosmetic effort designed to delay the day of reckoning? Indeed, key questions about the credibility of nation states as well as some institutions of the nation state will become major topic of global discourse.

The biggest threat that the global community faces today is that of globalization of economic failure. Experience has shown that economic failure is much easier to globalize than economic success. Economic success usually appears to contained in the country or region of origin but economic failure simply spreads like wild fire. A great deal of damage can be done across distant national boundaries within just twenty four hours. The way the major international stock exchanges respond to economic crisis is startling. It has the capacity to transmit shockwaves in all directions creating further anxiety for investors across the entire global landscape.

Indeed everybody desires to succeed economically in life, but economic success is impossible without economic survival. The majority of mankind is now thus primarily faced with the challenge of economic survival. Economic recessions lead to more economic hardship for most people. Unemployment levels shoot up and there is a reduction in the general quality of life for most people. This book was written to highlight how the general economic downturn can lead to personal or business bankruptcy. The way in which a national bankruptcy could lead to business and personal bankruptcy is also highlighted.

The concluding part of the book provide general tips and guidance for individuals, businesses and nations on how to craft economic survival plans in a given scenario of economic uncertainty. Because an economic recession is a direct threat to a stable lifestyle, it is vital that every individual is aware of its root causes, effects and measures required to survive it gracefully.

PART ONE

BACKGROUND HISTORY OF ECONOMIC CRISES

1. CHAPTER ONE: HISTORY OF THE GLOBAL ECONOMIC CRISES

2. CHAPTER TWO: THE GREAT DEPRESSION OF THE **1930's**

3. CHAPTER THREE: THE 2007/2008 GLOBAL FINANCIAL CRISIS

4. CHAPTER FOUR: THE LOOMING EUROPEAN SOVEREIGN DEBT CRISIS

CHAPTER ONE

History of Global Economic Crises

The 21st century is a period of rapid change in technology that has brought about an era of phenomenal change in the fortunes of nations, companies and individuals. The technological advancement recorded within the one hundred years of the 20th century prepared the ground for what is going on today. From the technological advancement that revolutionized transportation, telecommunications and business practices on a global scale to the significant progresses in human thought due to access to a richer source of information required for decision making.

In almost every field of human endeavor, significant progress has been recorded by people in all nations across the globe. More and more people are leveraging on technology to take advantage of the limitless opportunities in almost every nation of the world. More people are becoming wealthier at a faster rate. Mankind truly has a come into the Golden Age of Achievement.

Paradoxically, at the same time, the world is experiencing grave economic uncertainties. Corporate and national bankruptcies appear to be on the horizon. The curse of the fiscal irresponsibility has pushed mainly the developed nations to extreme levels of sovereign debts-sponsored spending that has become a threat to economic growth and recovery.

Trade imbalance amongst nations has created wide gaps in the economic lives of peoples and societies. The idea of free market economics with its penchant for free enterprise and free trade has simply produced disparate levels in the quality of lives of different people in different parts of the world.

The sovereign debt crisis facing the euro zone is a reflection of the failure of the implementation of the ideals of free market economics. Fiscal spending was not directed at growth enhancing activities in most countries. This led to a regime of low Gross Domestic Product growth rate in such economies. While emerging and developing economies were growing at higher rates in recent years, the developed economies of Europe and North America grew at slower rates. With the current debt crisis looming for the euro zone, GDP growth forecasts for these nations have been revised downwards by the International Monetary Fund (IMF).

The G20 nations, who account for 85% of the world's total GDP are mostly in Europe and North America. The current risk of economic crisis in Europe and North America has the potential to significantly affect economic performance of many other nations in Asia, South America and Africa.

Like individuals and companies, nation states are also involved a struggle for survival. The fact that the developed economies of the world are the ones deeply enmeshed in the current sovereign debt crisis proves that success in anything in life comes with a price tag. The questions begging for answers are thus:

1. What is the cost of Economic Success?
2. Who actually pays the price for this success?

Ii is important to note that before you can succeed either as an individual, a company or a nation – you must first of all survive.

Survival and success are therefore interlinked. Survival is a subset of success. Success includes survival.

Economic      Economic
Survival   Success

Figure1: Survival as a subset of success

The above figure suggests that survival needs are basic to all individuals, companies and nation states who desire economic growth and prosperity.

What then is Survival?

What are the survival needs

- Of the individual?
- Of the company?
- Of the nation state?

In September, 2011 the IMF Chief, **Christine Lagarde** warned that with the current euro zone debt crisis, the world economy is entering a dangerous phase. It was also mentioned that if the euro zone sovereign debt crisis is not properly managed, it could throw the entire global economy into another period of economic depression.

Economic depression is not new to world. The Great Depression of the 1930's transformed economic thinking. It led to an increase in government's involvement in the management of the economy. The Great Depression lasted between 1929 to the early 1940's. It was a period of significant economic decline and hardship for a vast majority of people in the United States of America and in many other market economies of the world.

Due to the hardship visited on individuals, families, businesses and communities during the Great Depression, it was indeed a turning point for most economies around the world. The level of economic destitution was so high in some countries that it led to a regime of political leadership changes across the globe. The economic view that governments must play an active role to stabilize demand in order to prevent further depressions gained ground.

In the United States, during the Great Depression it is estimated that more than a quarter of the working population became unemployed. A lot of people lost not only their investments but also their entire savings during the period. Farmers that were usually shielded during depressions were hit very hard by a serious drought that occurred during this period. Small farmers that were indebted did not only lose their harvest but their farms as well. Financial institutions had to foreclose on a lot of debtors.

The experience of the Great Depression is considered to be an immense tragedy for a vast majority of people that were directly affected. The massive job losses led to low consumer demand for goods. Debt defaults by individuals and businesses were high. Economic output was low and recovery was generally slow over the period.

Individuals and companies literally had to struggle to survive first. The challenge was to first and foremost provide for the basic physiological needs of individuals and families. Government programs were enacted to cater for the most vulnerable members of the society. The old and the aged, the unemployed, the young and those who had become indebted were bailed out by the government. Economic protectionist measures were sometimes adopted and this often led to counterproductive outcomes. Market confidence was eroded and political reforms were rampant.

The 2007-2008 global economic crises also impacted negatively on the entire global economy. Although, some historians are of the view that unlike the Great Depressions that was caused by global inadequate demand, the 2007-2008 economic crisis was caused by the housing bubble as well as the fragile financial system of the United States of America. Overcoming the 2007-2008 global economic crises was costly for most nations. The extent of exposure to the dynamics of world economy affected the cost of recovery at different levels for different nations. It became obvious that the extent of dependence and economic integration with other nations is a determining factor of how shocks and failures in a foreign economy affect another domestic economy.

The looming 2011 Sovereign Debt Crisis is unprecedented in the history of the global economy. It is in fact a new frame of experience whose ripple effects have not been fully appreciated. Credit rating agencies have been downgrading the sovereign debt status of many European nations as well as that of the United States of America. It's been argued that unlike the previous economic crisis, the current one is being fuelled by fiscal irresponsibility on the part of governments.

In most of the countries risking a sovereign debt default, over the years, expansionary fiscal spending of governments was done with debt financing. The ratio of loan to GDP increased rapidly to the point whereby debt repayment obligations now threaten the ability of nation states to invest in growth enhancing expenditure projects.

It is in light of the above that it is considered necessary to do a simple review of the impact of global economic recessions on nations, businesses and individual within the global economy.

Individuals, households, businesses and nation states must ensure their own economic survival before they can even dream about success in uncertain economic climes. To achieve both in an interdependent world, it means that adequate preparation must be made for the challenges ahead.

CHAPTER TWO

The Great Depression of the 1930's

On Tuesday the 29th of October in 1929, the American stock market crashed. This day is often referred to by historians and economists as Black Tuesday. The stock market crash of 29th October, 1929 marked the official commencement of the Great Depressions that would last up to the early 1940's.

The period of 1929 to the early 1940's during which the Great Depression lasted was marked by severe economic hardship for most nations of the world. Personal, business and government bankruptcies were widespread. Unemployment increases impacted negatively on consumer spending. This consequently affected businesses and industrial productivity. Economic growth declined across most nations of the world.

In the United States of America, over 25% of people were out of work. Workers and farmers lost heavily from their savings and investments. Individuals and households who had lost almost everything of value that they owned roamed the country in search of sustenance.

A new wave of political change ushered in new economic reforms such as the New Deal that was designed to improve the American economy. Governments across the world took a more serious role in economic management. Social security and unemployment compensation was introduced to reduce the hardships faced by the vulnerable members of society. New models of economic thinking emerged in order to chart new courses of action required to deal with the crisis.

From the United States of America to Great Britain, France, Germany and many other nations of the world, there was a general decline in industrial production, wholesale prices and foreign trade. Unemployment statistics shot up to unprecedented levels. The entire economic environment of most countries became unfavorable.

Causes of the Great Depression of the 1930's

So far, the Great Depression is still being regarded as the worst economic recession that the world has suffered. In the United States, historians have provided a lot of arguments on the causes of the Great Depression. Although no consensus has been reached on a list of causes, the following represent some of the reasons that have been advanced:

1. The Stock Market Crash of 1929
2. Bank Failures and Liquidation
3. The Dust Bowl/Drought of the 1930's
4. US Protectionism
5. Reductions in consumer spending
6. Weak financial system regulatory framework
7. Weak government participation in the economy
8. Productivity shock preceding the 1929 stock market crash.

1. The Stock Market Crash of 1929

Prior to the Black Tuesday of 29th October in 1929, stock prices on Wall Street began to fall around 4th September 1929. But the experience of Black Tuesday left an indelible mark on the confidence of investors in the stock market. It appeared as if the crashing stock prices had no end in sight, confidence in the market was at an all time low.

There was panic selling of stocks in a climate where there was no demand. Stock prices continued to crash amidst the uncertainty and confusion created in the market. Suddenly, it seemed as though one of the surest ways of becoming wealthy in the United States through the stock market was indeed but a big pipe dream.

The crash of the stock market quickly set in motion a chain of events that would later serve to worsen the general economic climate. It is therefore understandable that economic historians refer to Black Tuesday as the official commencement of the Great Depression. This is despite the fact that evidences abound as to the existence of other symptoms of an economic depression prior to the 29th October 1929. Black Tuesday remains the single most significant day whose events precipitated the full onset of the Great Depression.

Investor/market confidence, business failures, consumer spending, employment levels and productivity were all impacted negatively by the Stock Market Crash. These problems in the United States economy were quickly transmitted to other market economies of the world and the entire global economy went into a depression.

Figure 2: Effects of the Stock Market Crash

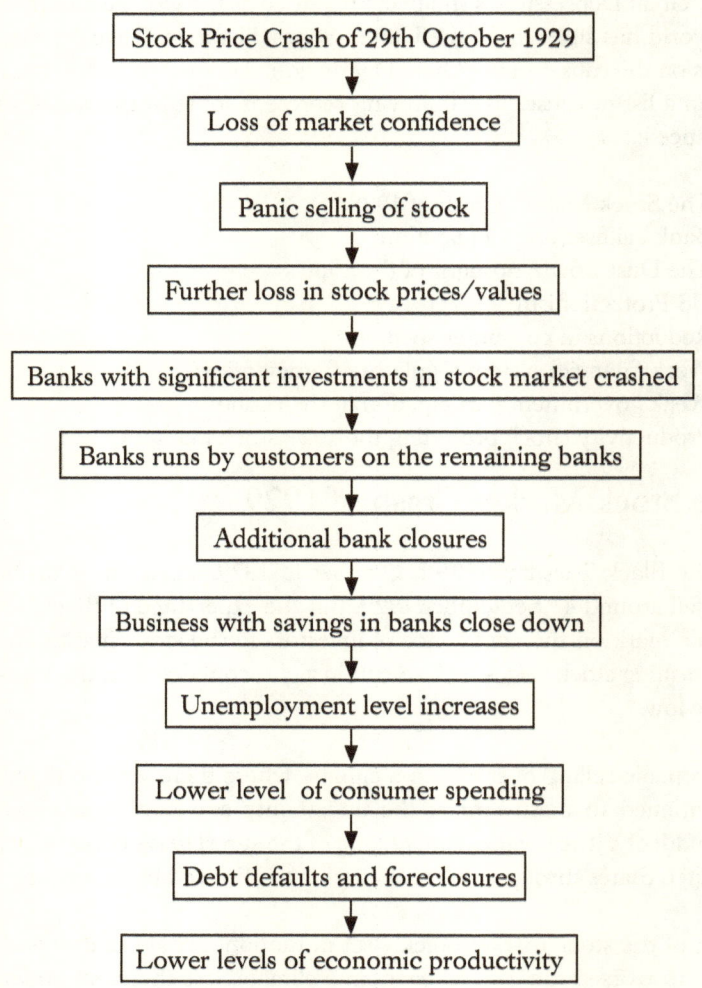

2.   Bank Failures and Liquidation

The regulatory environment for the financial services sector in most countries was weak prior to the Great Depression. Uninsured bank deposits led to significant loss of savings by depositors. Banks that had invested heavily in the stock market folded up following the stock market crash in the United States.

The spate of bank failures led to bank runs on the existing banks. Large withdrawals by depositors created liquidity problems for most of the banks. Subsequently more banks went under as a result of the liquidity challenges. The banks that were left became cautious. Such banks refused to grant new loans to businesses and individuals. A new era of liquidity squeeze for businesses and individuals was on the horizon.

Bank and business failures meant that more and more people remain out of work. During the Great Depression of the 1930's, it is estimated that over 9000 (Nine Thousand) banks failed in the United States of America alone. The massive unemployment created by bank and business failures impacted negatively on consumer spending. Individuals and businesses focused on survival needs. People generally avoided the luxury goods segments of the economy.

3.   The Dust Bowl/ The Drought of the 1930's

Economic depressions usually compel people to focus on the basic survival needs of food, shelter and clothing. It is therefore natural that farmers who grow and deal in agricultural produce are partly shielded from the crisis. This is because it is assumed that at least they can continue to feed their families. This was not however the case during the Great Depression of the 1930's.

During this period, the Great Plains was hit by serious drought and dust storms. Farmers lost their crops to the weather conditions. The effect of this drought in the Mississippi valley in the 1930 left a lot of farmers indebted. Eventually, some had to sell their farms or had them taken over by financial institutions. Small farmers in large numbers were particularly affected.

It is important to note that the drought was not a direct cause of the Great Depression. But the timing of its incidence in the 1930's worsened an already bad economic situation. The tragedy was compounded as people starved and wandered around the country in search of greener pasture.

4. US Protectionism

To protect the United States economy following the business failures that occurred at the early stages of the depression, the US government created the Smoot-Hawley Tariff in 1930. This tariff increased taxes on imports and was intended to protect domestic American enterprises.

Subsequently, there was a reduction in the volume of trade between the United States of America and its other trading partners. In addition to reductions in trade volumes, some countries retaliated by placing high taxes on imported goods from the United States of America. The net effect of the US protectionist measures was thus counterproductive to the US economy.

The spread of the Great Depression to other parts of the world from the United States was compounded by the reduction in international trade following the introduction of the US protectionist measures. In the late 1920's international trade was a small fraction of the US overall economic activity. But it was a major part of the economic activities of many other nations that traded with the United States.

With the introduction of the Smoot-Hawley Tariff Act in June 17 1930, American-bound exports became more expensive. Foreign countries imposed retaliatory tariffs on American-manufactured goods. This trend led of significant decline in the global level of international trade.

Farm exports collapsed in the United States with commodities like cotton, tobacco and wheat being seriously affected. Farmers and businesses defaulted on loan obligations leading to further depression within the economy.

5. Reductions in Consumer Spending

The stock market crash of 29th October 1929 affected the ability of individuals, banks and businesses to access cash for their expenditure needs. Stock certificates became worthless pieces of paper that no buyer was willing to take up. Both the rich and poor within the American society simply stopped making new purchases. Most of expenditure was directed at meeting basic survival needs of individuals, households and companies. The fact that consumer spending went down meant that less money was available to businesses from sales. Companies ended up producing fewer products. Companies shrank and laid-off employees. More unemployment created more debt defaults by employees that had gone out of employment.

Individual debt defaults coupled with the gradual build of unsold stocks in the stores and factories compounded the situation. The fact is that during this period of economic uncertainty, individuals and companies practically had little or no access to liquidity and banks were no longer optimistic about granting new loans and credit facilities to either individuals or companies.

6. Weak Financial System Regulation Framework

The bank failures in the United States of America led to loss of money in billions of dollars. It is reported that soon after the stock market crash of 1929 and during the months of January to October in 1930, Seven Hundred and Forty Four (744) United States financial institutions failed. It is estimated that Nine Thousand (9000) US financial institutions failed during the period of the Great Depression. What really was responsible for the massive failure of institutions within the financial system?

The stock market crash led to multiple runs by depositors on banks. Business failures and falling income levels meant that outstanding debt obligations had become more expensive. Debt defaults as well as uninsured deposits with the banks could not be adequately covered by government guarantees.

During the period preceding the stock market crash, there was a near absence or rather ineffective Federal Reserve banking regulations to deal with the scenario of massive bank runs. With non-performing loans heavily pulling down their performance in the face of an uncertain economic future, financial institutions invested less in the real economy. Almost every corporate entity was principally concerned about its own survival.

For the first time governments across the globe appreciated the need for greater government involvement in the economy as well as taking up greater responsibility for protecting the most vulnerable segments of society.

7. Weak Government Participation in the Economy

The New York Bank of the United States is one of the largest bank failures that opened the floodgates for many other banks to subsequently fall. The stance of the Federal Reserve at that time was also viewed to have contributed to the onset of the Great Depression.

It is also argued that monetary contraction that was a consequence of improper policy measures of the Federal Reserve at that time exacerbated the depression. The Federal Reserve was accused to shrinking aggregate money supply within the American economy in addition to inaction in the face of a serious liquidity crisis in the banking industry. This led to a heightened period of multiple bank runs and massive bank failures.

Government involvement in the economy was considered weak. Emergency or short-term lending windows were not extended to the banks. Bailout funds were not made available. The Federal Reserve took no serious measures to increase the money supply within the American economy.

With this situation, it became practically impossible for businesses and individuals to pay back their existing loans. New investments were almost frozen. Ongoing investment projects with long term horizon suffered.

Government's ability to intervene in the crisis was limited by regulations through the Federal Reserve Act. The Federal Reserve Act limited the amount of credit the Federal Reserve could issue. This limitation required 40% gold backing for all the currency notes that the Federal Reserve issued. This credit limit had almost been exhausted prior to the stock market crash of 1929. Following this experience, governments had to take a more active role in the management of money supply within the economy in line with the desired level of overall economic activity.

It is widely viewed that weak action or inaction of the Federal Reserve transformed a normal economic recession into the Great Depression of the 1930's.

8. Productivity Shock

Advancements in technology ushered in an era of industrialization in the beginning of the 20th century. Motorization, electrification and industrialization led to a significant boom in productivity on a global scale. Suddenly, machines were producing more and more goods, much more than men could afford to buy or consume at that time. The rate of output growth was so fast that it created large growing piles of unsold stock in many warehouses leading to a situation often regarded as productivity shock.

The heavy investment in industrial capacity is significant of the unrestricted accumulation of capital in a free market setting. The increase in output was not matched by a corresponding increase in wages and income. Because income growth was not at parity with output, the demand for goods and services was well below the supply.

With insufficient demand for goods, it meant that businesses held high levels of unsold stock. Increasing stock levels in a liquidity-starved economic environment meant more business failures and thus economic recession.

According to Karl Marx, the only restriction to the accumulation of capital under free-market capitalism is the market itself. Since no one controls the market except the market itself, it is inevitable that an economic crisis in the mould of recession or a depression will result from the unrestricted accumulation of capital.

From the above, it is instructive to note that an economic recession may occur after a period of prosperity. The factors that lead to a recession are inherently built up during times of economic prosperity. In fact, it is when due care and attention is not paid to these risk factors that they are transformed to expose an economy to a recession.

Effects of the Great Depression

The Great Depressions of the 1930's led to the following general trend in most countries across the globe. In some countries, the effect was mild while in others it was severe.

1. A reduction in the personal income levels of individuals.
2. A reduction in governments' collected tax revenue.
3. A reduction in the profits of companies, businesses and corporate entities.
4. A general fall in wholesale prices for goods and services.
5. A reduction in the general level of international trade for most countries.
6. An increase in unemployment levels.
7. Construction and capital expenditure shrink significantly and in many countries were stopped altogether.
8. Cash crop farming suffered leading to the collapse of farm exports.
9. Bank and business failures led to economic destitution for individuals and households.
10. Industrial production shrinks in order to match output to effective demand for goods during the period.

Effects On Some Nation States

The Great Depression of the 1930's left an indelible mark on the political and economic history of many nation states. A summary of the some of the effects for different nations is highlighted below:

CANADA

The Canadian economy during the Great Depression was strongly affected by events in the United States. Canada was indeed affected by both the global economic downturn as well as the drought conditions of the period.

The total income fell to almost half of the 1929 level by 1932. Unemployment was estimated to cover more than a quarter of the working population. The 1932 level of industrial production was short by 42% of the 1929 level.

The unemployed marched through the major cities of Canada. In addition to the closure of businesses, farmers experienced hard times during the period.

FRANCE

France was not so quickly affected by the Depression until sometime around 1931. The economy was relatively self-reliant and with a limited level of dependence on the global economy. Unemployment increased during the period.

GERMANY

To date, Germany remains the single most referred to example of what could happen to the political life of a country in the aftermath of a period of severe economic hardship.

Political extremism sometimes is fuelled by economic hardship. The Great Depression of the 1930's prepared the grounds for the rise of Adolf Hitler to power and the eventual commencement of the Second World War in 1939.

Before then, Germany was dependent on American loans for economic transformation. The economic crisis in the United States especially beginning from the 1929 market crash as well as the monetary contraction by the Federal Reserve meant that those sources of loan financing were drying up. Germany was deeply affected by the American situation. More and more people became unemployed and the rate of unemployment was reported to have peaked 30% in 1932.

The economic hardship in Germany fuelled the nationalistic ideals of Adolf Hitler and this eventually brought this Nazi Party to power in Germany 1933. The Second World War officially began in 1939 and the rest is history.

JAPAN

Japan is a very good example of a nation state that was mildly affected by the Great Depressions of the 1930's. In addition, the experience of Japan is also a good example of how fiscal stimulus and currency devaluation could be used to mitigate the negative impact of an economic recession.

Fiscal stimulus was introduced through a host of measures including deficit spending. The industrial production was doubled during the 1930's. The measures adopted by the Japanese authorities were so effective to the point that by 1933 the country had emerged from the economic depression. In fact, by 1934 the Japanese economy was poised to overheat. In a bid to avoid inflationary trends, fiscal spending had to be immediately reduced.

SOUTH AFRICA

South Africa is another good example of how economic hardship can give rise to the blossoming of nationalist or extremist ideals in the political landscape of nations.

The Apartheid system of racial segregation has its roots in some of the experiences of the Great Depression. South Africa was dependant on its solid minerals and agricultural exports. The crash in the volume of international trade meant that the income of the government from these sources took a major hit.

Economic hardship and destitution from the depression caused social and racial segregation. This impacted negatively on the future realignment of political forces which later paved the way for the emergence of the apartheid system of government in the future.

SOVIET UNION

The Soviet Union, ideologically shield from the global market economy was mildly affected by the Great Depression. Because the principles of free market capitalism were not in force in this environment, it remained effectively shielded from the economic crisis at that time.

UNITED KINGDOM

The United Kingdom had a bag of mixed economic experiences in different regions and different sectors of the UK economy during the period.

For instance, in areas such as the Midlands and South of England, the effects of the depression lasted for only a very short time. The later years of the 1930's was a period of economic prosperity cutting through the agriculture and manufacturing sectors.

However, the industrial northern part of the UK was severely affected by the Great Depression. Exports of goods from this region had fallen by more than half by the end of 1930. Unemployment in this region was reported to have peaked 20% of the insured workforce at the end of 1930. The rates of unemployment were significantly higher in certain cities of the region.

UNITED STATES OF AMERICA

The impact of the Great Depression on the US economy is well chronicled. Unemployment peaked at 25% by 1933. Businesses, households and individuals that were dependent on agriculture were undergoing serious economic hardship from the severe drought of the 1930's. Loan defaults by businesses and individuals had become common. Large populations of homeless people wandering across the country could be found in shanty towns or ghettos called "Hoovervilles". This was the period of President Herbert Hoover.

Apparently, President Hoover's policies failed to address the worsening conditions of the American economy. The implementation of the Smoot-Hawley Tariff Act of 1930 which was designed to promote the consumption of American goods subsequently led to a retaliatory backlash from America's trading partners. All of which contributed to deepen the Depression.

The failure of President Hoover's economic policies to address the depression led to the emergence of Franklin Deland Roosevelt as the President of the United States in 1932. The new government was not only facing the economic challenges of the period but equally had to contend with the serious drought and erosion that was experienced shortly after coming into office.

President Roosevelt introduced the New Deal which is a series of economic programs designed to promote financial systems stability, stimulate consumer demand and provide reliefs and work for the vulnerable segments of society.

A number of economic reforms were thus implemented across board. Fiscal stimulus was provided in strategic sectors of the economy. Social security, housing and unemployment compensation were attended to. Some of the terms associated with the New Deal programs include the following:

CCC – Civilian Conservation Corps
AAA – Agricultural Adjustment Administration
WPA – Works Progress Administration
NRA – National Recovery Administration

CHAPTER THREE

The 2007/2008 Global Financial Crisis

The global financial crisis of 2007 and 2008 was caused by a combination of factors chief amongst which is the mortgage slump in the United States. Prior to the housing crisis, subprime mortgages had been extended to a large number of borrowers with weak credit status. Over time, it became difficult to recover the mortgages extended to the subprime lenders and this precipitated the eventual freeze of credit when there was a massive flight of the capital by investors.

Lucjan T. Orlowski of the Department of Economics and Finance, Sacred Heart University Fairfield Connecticut, USA in a discussion paper titled; Stages of the 2007/2008 Global Financial Crisis: Is there a wandering asset price bubble? The following five distinctive stages of the crisis were identified namely:

Stage 1:   The outbreak of the subprime mortgage crisis.
Stage 2:   The proliferation of credit risk along with the broadening of losses of financial institutions.
Stage 3:   The eruption of liquidity crisis heightened by the run on Bear Stearns with the spread of contagion effects on other investment banks with similar portfolio characteristics (most notably, Lehman Brothers).
Stage 4:   The commodity price bubble.
Stage 5:   The ultimate freeze of credit markets accompanied by the massive flight of safety by investors.

It is instructive to note that both micro-economic and systemic factors created a situation whereby the US housing market was overpriced and poorly regulated. The excess liquidity within the US economy and in the hands of banks created an attitude of aggressive investments by banks in the mortgages housing market.

The US housing market crash created serious challenges to the financial institutions in terms of management of the types of financial risks that arose from the situation.

The housing bubble spread beyond mortgages into other classes of assets, specialized investment banks and universal banks. The highly exposed banks to the mortgage crisis immediately experienced massive withdrawals of liabilities from their portfolios. This was the commencement of the global liquidity crisis following the housing slump. Lehman Brothers, Bear Stearns and Northern Rock experienced runs. Anxiety and uncertainty about the risk of exposure to credits then led to the spread of the liquidity crisis across other nations of the world.

Sources of credit virtually dried up as financial institutions adopted a conservative attitude to lending. Investors generally held on to what they had as a result of the pessimism that has been created by economic uncertainty.

With credit and investments on a downward slide, global economic growth was threatened. Nations had to rely on the reserves they had built up over the years to augment revenue shortfalls. Where there was no augmentation of revenue shortfalls, there was less investments/spending in economic infrastructure hence less economic growth.

Some Causes of the 2007/2008 Global Financial Crisis

The housing market in the United States prior to year 2007 experienced a gradual boom supported by new financial product innovations by the financial institutions. Mortgages were securitized and structured as financial products were introduced. When the housing market collapsed due to macroeconomic and systemic faults, some of the following reasons were advanced as root causes of the crisis:

1. A global savings glut
2. Excessive liquidity created by the U.S. Federal Reserve
3. Excessive creation of credit by financial institutions
4. Proliferation of subprime mortgages
5. Violations of total debt service safety standards for mortgages
6. Difficulty in financial risk assessments by the financial institutions
7. Wrong credit rating assessments
8. Excessive leverage (borrowing) by banks.

Figure 3: Some Root Causes of the 2007/2008 Global Financial Crisis

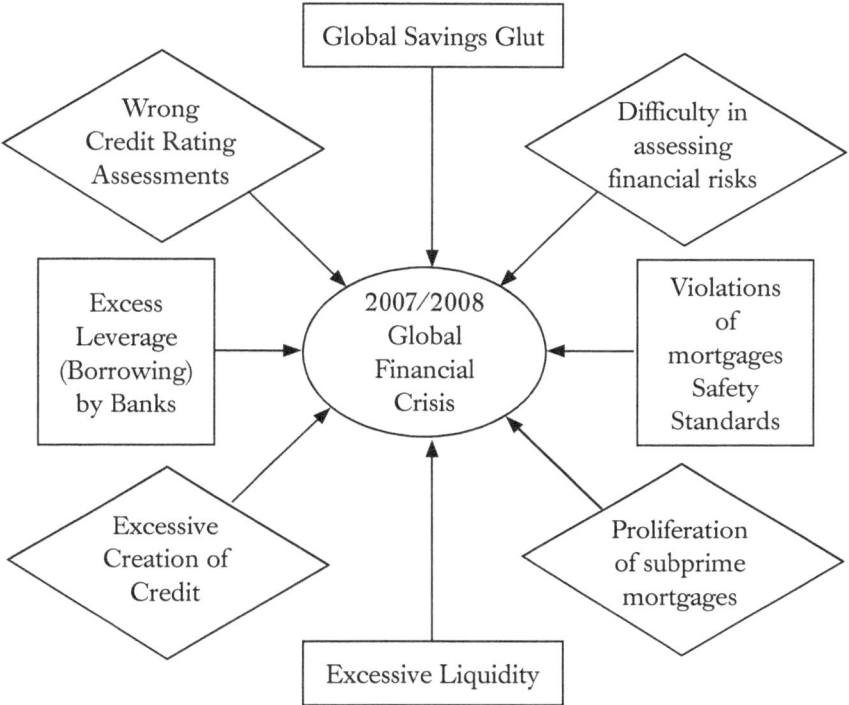

The Case of Iceland

Beginning from the year 2008, Iceland has been undergoing major economic and political crisis following the collapse of the country's banking industry. To avoid a national bankruptcy, three of the country's major commercial banks were placed into receivership in 2008. The banks could not refinance their shot-term debts in addition to other serious liquidity challenges that led to their bankruptcy.

The collapse of Iceland's banking industry had negative multiplier effects on the economy. The currency suffered in value. The stock market was negatively impacted and international trade declined. The country was thrown into a serious phase of economic recession.

It is reported that from January to September 2008, the Icelandic currency (Krona) depreciated by more than 35% in value relative to the Euro. Inflation had also hit double digit.

The Nordic Iceland Exchange initially had stock trading suspended for some financial institutions in October 2008. As a result of panic selling of shares that was driving down stock prices, share trading in the exchange was put on hold for two days by the authorities. Market conditions extended the period of closing until 14th October when the market was opened to the public. By then the value of equities and total market capitalization had been seriously impacted negatively.

With negative future ratings for Iceland's sovereign debt by the rating agencies, the economic situation was compounded. Debt had become a much larger proportion of the country's GDP and the country was running a deficit budget.

Business and individual bankruptcies were experienced in Iceland. For instance, Sterling Airlines declared bankruptcy on October 29 2008. This is in addition to many other economic and corporate reforms cutting across industries in Iceland. More people were thrown out of work as a result of the bankruptcies.

Importation of goods was restricted to a few products as the government lacked sufficient reserves to support imports. Asset values for businesses contracted and inflation made the situation worse.

The crisis in Iceland created a lot of concern for some UK local authorities and organizations that had invested heavily in the Icelandic banks. The safety and security of the investments and deposits became an issue of grave concern.

The Parliament of Iceland eventually had to pass the Icesave Bill in order to avoid retaliation from the United Kingdom and Netherlands. The bill was passed on 28th August 2009 for the purpose of repaying the United Kingdom and Netherlands over $5billion (Five Billion US Dollars) that had been lost as deposits in the bank accounts of Iceland's banks.

The failure of the major banks in Iceland kick-started a series of criminal investigations against banks and business leaders. High profile arrests were made of some suspects and a lot of prominent business and industry leaders of Iceland have been placed on a watch list.

The political climate was also affected by the financial crisis of Iceland. Some politicians were fingered in having received unconventional loans from the banks without adequate security. The public staged protests against the government and its organs for lack of responsibility in the course of the crisis.

Diplomatic ripples between Iceland on one side and Britain, Denmark and Sweden occurred. The International Monetary Fund was not also spared by the Icelandic authorities.

Eventually, the Prime Minister of Iceland, **Geir H. Harde** had to tender the resignation of the government to the President. The failure of Iceland's political leaders to agree on a common approach to tackle the financial crisis led to many high profile resignations and layoffs eventually precipitating the collapse of the government. Iceland is still struggling to emerge from this financial crisis that started in 2008 as at 2011. The case of Iceland is a good example of what could happen to a nation as well as its trading and investment partners in the event of a national bankruptcy. The impact on the economic life of individuals and households could indeed be severe.

CHAPTER FOUR

The Looming European Sovereign Debt Crisis

The rising cost of sovereign debt in some European countries has fuelled global fears about the looming prospect of a sovereign debt crisis that could trigger another global financial crisis. The following European countries have all witnessed a steady increase in the cost of their sovereign debts in the last one year:

1. Greece
2. Portugal
3. Ireland
4. Hungary
5. Italy
6. Spain
7. Belgium
8. France
9. Germany
10. United Kingdom

The case of Greece appears to be the most imminent and talked about. Concerns about the spread of the euro zone sovereign debt crisis spreading to other parts of the world have also been on the front burner of financial and economic discourse.

Reflecting on the experience of Iceland which is relatively a small country in size, it is inconceivable what bigger crises might ensue from economically larger and more strategic nations of the euro zone. It has been argued that a single national bankruptcy in the euro zone has the capacity to threaten the economies all the other nations of the European Union and by extension the Euro currency itself.

The contagion effect is likely to quickly extend to the United States of America. The global economy is thus at risk with the fragile financial system of the United States of America. The US Dollar as a currency of international exchange will also be threatened. The multiplier effect of a sovereign debt crisis across the world is worst imagined. In the words of International Monetary Fund Boss; **Christine Lagarde**, the looming sovereign debt crisis has brought the world closer to 'a new dangerous phase'.

Should a financial crisis break out from a sovereign debt default, it is clear that the investments, deposits, trade and asset values that will be affected will cut across many nations of the world. The multidimensional effect of the failure of the financial system in one country will no doubt have serious impacts on individuals and businesses in many other countries that have some level of economic partnership or dependence with the bankrupt nation.

Historical Origins of the Crisis

It is strongly argued that the looming sovereign debt crisis had its origins from the recent 2007/2008 global financial crisis. As a result of the 2007/2008 global financial crisis, there was credit freeze across many nations of the world. Most governments had to bail out banks in the financial system. To do this, they operated deficit budgets and incurred increasing amounts of sovereign debts to finance the fiscal deficits.

The sharp increase in bank bail out over the years meant that sovereign debts were increasing as government deficits continued to rise. Over time, this led to a crisis of confidence by investors who had become conscious of the fact that increasing levels of sovereign debts could negatively impact on a nation's ability to honors debt repayment obligations as at when due. This was especially worrisome in a situation whereby the national GDP growth was not flattering. This anxiety affected the cost of acquiring further sovereign debts for the affected countries.

Measures adopted by most of the countries to cut fiscal spending met with a lot of resistance from the citizenry. Public protests have been recently reported in Greece. The European Union, concerned about the possible impact of a sovereign debt default on the region came up with measures to stabilize the region.

The European Financial Stability Facility (EFSF) which is a comprehensive financial rescue facility for the region was approved by Europe's Finance Ministers on 9th May 2011. The looming sovereign debt crisis is thought to be more likely in the nation states of Greece, Ireland and Portugal. However, the possible spread of the financial crisis to the other nations of the world is real. Economic leaders of the world have been speaking on the need for this imminent crisis to be contained by the euro zone.

In recent times, virtually all the nations of the euro zone have had their sovereign debt status downgraded by all the major international credit rating agencies. This is in addition to the downgrading of the 2011 economic outlook of the entire euro zone region by the IMF.

Figure 4: **Origins of the Looming European Sovereign Debt Crisis**

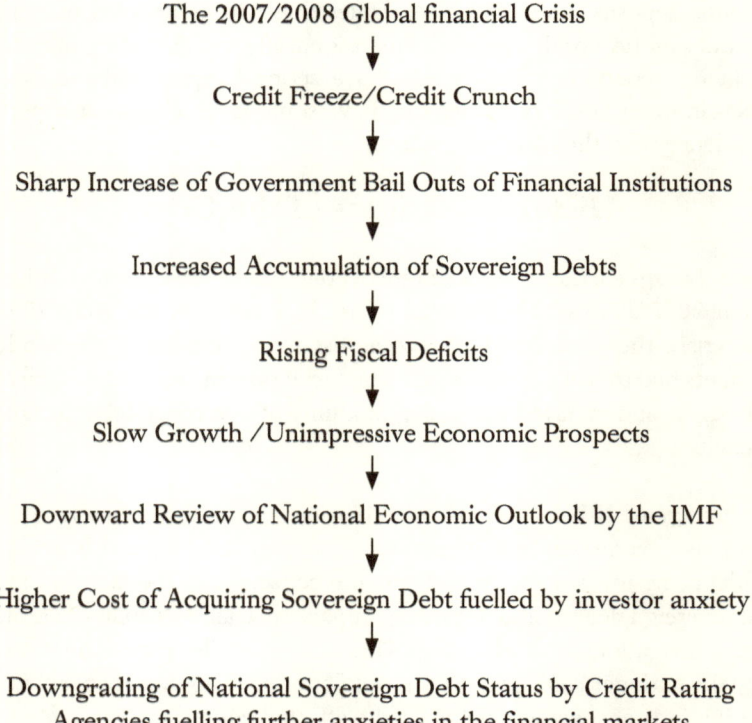

The 2007/2008 Global financial Crisis
↓
Credit Freeze/Credit Crunch
↓
Sharp Increase of Government Bail Outs of Financial Institutions
↓
Increased Accumulation of Sovereign Debts
↓
Rising Fiscal Deficits
↓
Slow Growth /Unimpressive Economic Prospects
↓
Downward Review of National Economic Outlook by the IMF
↓
Higher Cost of Acquiring Sovereign Debt fuelled by investor anxiety
↓
Downgrading of National Sovereign Debt Status by Credit Rating Agencies fuelling further anxieties in the financial markets

From the beginning of the year 2010 to date, a lot of attention has been focused on Greece and other European countries caught in this sovereign debt crisis.

In May 2010, the International Monetary Fund proposed harsh austerity measures for Greece as conditions for a €110 billion (One Hundred and Ten Billion Euro) loan. Ireland and Portugal were also given IMF rescue bail-outs in the sums of €85 billion (Eighty Five Billion Euros) and €78 billion (Seventy Eight Billion Euros) respectively.

Refinancing or restructuring of Greece's public debt has been a major challenge since the onset of the crisis. Access to further sovereign credit from financiers at a fair cost is still a challenge while the lender of last resort is providing harsh austerity terms for additional bailout packages. The austerity measures proposed by the Greek government only met with public resistance as protests increased in frequency.

Being the very first crisis that the euro zone is facing since its creation in 1999, it is instructive to be vigilant to the lessons inherent in the experience.

Possible Spread of Crisis and Other Concerns

Fears of a possible spread of the European sovereign debt crisis have been rife in all parts of the world. The experience from the recent United States debt ceiling debacle is still fresh on the memory of many watchers. On 2nd August 2011, the US Government narrowly missed a sovereign debt default with the American Congress approving to raise sovereign debt ceilings for the government. However, market capitalization of the major international stock exchanges took a hit while the debate lasted as to whether or not to approve an increase in US debt ceiling levels.

During the 2007/2008 global financial crisis, the key question on the minds of many observers was whether the global financial system itself was credible. Governments averted a serious crisis of confidence in the financial system by bailing out a lot of banks and providing fiscal stimulus programs for different sectors of the economy. In effect, most government's dealt with the symptoms of the crisis rather than the root causes. In addition, governments also took measures to forestall against the complete erosion of confidence in the financial system that is so central to the maintenance of order and discipline in financial markets.

When businesses also fail the credibility of the company's leadership has always been called to question. But what happens when there is a national bankruptcy? The experience of Iceland suggests that the entire political leadership of any country that becomes bankrupt is at risk.

Already, analysts and commentators are already asking the same question in all countries that are at the risk of sovereign debt default. Politics affects the nature of financial regulations in place. Political partisanship sometime delays the process of decision making at the legislative arm of governments. In matters of serious economic importance, it is vital that political leaders are able to be less-partisan and act quickly to safeguard general economic interests.

Recently, the role of political partisanship in the management of the economy has come under great scrutiny. When opposition political parties to the governments in power are strong, the tendency for quick passage of legislations required for economic development becomes low. In search of excuses to de-market the government in power, the opposition seizes such opportunities the score cheap political points and thus undermine the efforts of the government in power.

It is therefore instructive to be able to distinguish clearly between vital economic issues and partisan issues. The role of the political leadership of a nation is central to economic survival and success.

It has been argued by some analysts that what has just happened with the looming sovereign debt crisis is the amplification of the 2007/2008 global financial crisis from a financial system crisis to a national economic crisis. Governments' efforts rather than arresting the root causes of the 2007/2008 crisis simply provided short term palliative measures. It was therefore held that the crisis was bound to rebound once the tipping point of each economy is reached.

In most instances there was irresponsible expansion of government fiscal deficits. The clamor for responsible governance in society is a major feature in many countries today. A key attribute of responsible political leadership is living within the means of the government. If sovereign debt is required to fund critical government expenditures, it must be done with the highest sense of responsibility.

An Unfolding Scenario: GREECE

Greece as a member of the euro zone contributes about two point five percent (2.5%) to the entire economy of the euro zone. In size this might appear small. But in relative importance to other euro zone economies, it is quite significant.

As a member of the euro zone economy, Greece cannot on its own use monetary policy to stimulate its economy. The Greek government cannot simply inject or withdraw money from the economy, unless of course Greece chooses to exit from the euro zone. In such a situation, it can then be responsible for its own currency and perhaps use a host of monetary policy measures to regulate the supply of its currency within and outside its economy.

Greece is at the forefront of all the countries expected to slip into the sovereign debt default crisis. Greece had a strong economy and grew at an annual rate of 4.2%

between years 2000 to 2007. The cost of borrowing during the period was quite low and the government financed large fiscal deficits using cheap loans acquired during the period.

It is reported that the 2007/2008 global financial crisis heavily impacted on the shipping and tourism industry in Greece. These two industries are some of the most prominent in Greece. It is equally reported that the government of Greece in a bid to hide the true level of government deficit had over the years underreported the country's official economic statistics.

In year 2009 and 2010, the government of Greece carried out an upward review of its deficits reaching 13.6% relative to the Gross Domestic Product. At this time, this figure (13.6%) represents one of the highest deficits to GDP ratios in the world.

According to a publication on Wikipedia.org titled: European Sovereign Debt Crisis, the debt owed by the Greek government was estimated to be €216 Billion (Two Hundred and Sixteen Billion Euros) in January 2010.

In April 2010 the credit rating agency, Standard and Poor's downgraded the Greek government's debt rating in view of heightened fears of a likely default. There were concerns about Greece's ability as a nation to refinance its debt. With this situation, stock markets across the globe took a hit.

Other international rating agencies also downgraded the Greek government's debt rating. The net effect of the above downgrades was an increase in Greek bond yields. The Greek bond yields have thus continued to rise upwards in consequence of the lower debt ratings thereby making it more costly for the Greek government to acquire more debts.

Chronology of some key Events in Greece

1. 5th March 2010: The Economic Protection Bill was passed by the Greek Parliament. The purpose of the Bill was to save about €5 billion (Five Billion Euros) through a collection of measures which included wage slashes of public sector workers.

2. 23rd April 2010: The Greek Government requested that the European Union/International Monetary Fund bailout package for Greece be put

into action. It was held that the government of Greece needed to have funds before the 19th day of May 2010 or face a debt rollover.

3.   2nd May 2010: A major loan agreement was reached between Greece, other countries of the euro zone and the International Monetary Fund. A total of €110 billion (One Hundred and Ten Billion Euros) was agreed with €45 billion (Forty Five billion Euros) of this sum as immediate loans.

4.   5th May 2010: In protest to the planned austerity programs that the Greek government was about to impose, a nationwide strike was held. The austerity programs were intended to increase taxation as well as reduce government expenditure in certain areas.

A tripartite committee known as the **Troika** was set up by the European Commission, the International Monetary Fund and the European Central Bank. The role of Troika was to broker a bailout package for the Greece government in exchange for some conditions/terms from the euro zone contributor nations.

The Challenges for Greece

The nation state of Greece, with high levels of sovereign debt as well as high fiscal deficit is faced with the issue of a rapidly increasing cost of acquiring new sovereign debts. It seems inevitable that a sovereign debt default is likely unless a long-term, comprehensive and affordable bailout agreement is reached.

It is estimated that there is 25% to 90% probability of a Greek debt default or restructuring. In a default there would be some debt restructuring where creditors such as the IMF and euro zone countries will receive part of the €110 billion that they are owed. Because only part of this loan and many others may be recovered, the default has the tendency to undermine the European financial markets.

To access cheaper funding from its European partners, Greece had to agree to some harsh conditions which included imposing a host of austerity measures. These austerity measures have led to public protests and civil unrests. Greece as such has to strike a healthy balance between the negative economic and social consequences of imposing the austerity measures on one hand and the economic benefits of cheaper borrowing from its euro zone partners.

The Vicious Cycle of Bankruptcies

An examination of the causes and effects of bankruptcies in the case of individuals, businesses and nations reveals a vicious cycle of cause and effect. If unchecked, personal bankruptcies have the tendency to create business bankruptcies which in turn can precipitate a national bankruptcy. Not only is there a cause and effect pattern, the trend of impact works both ways.

Figure 5: The Vicious cycle of Bankruptcies

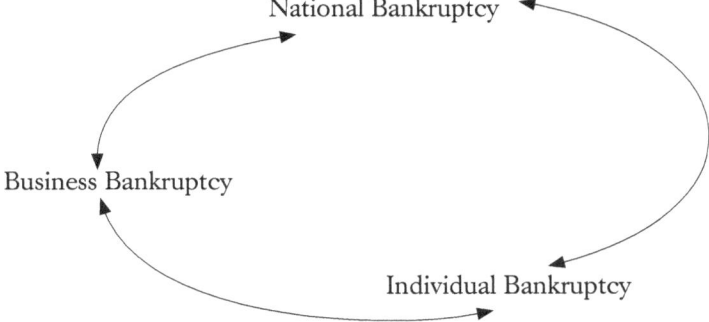

PART TWO

BANKRUPTCY AND THE INDIVIDUAL, THE BUSINESS AND THE NATIONAL ECONOMY

CHAPTER FIVE

Personal/Individual Bankruptcy

Personal bankruptcy occurs when an individual is unable to pay debt obligations as at when due. This may occur when an individual loses his source of income or mismanages the funds/income at his disposal.

An individual faced with such a situation will naturally seek for a restructuring of his/her debt payment obligations with creditors or alternatively seek for protection under the Bankruptcy Act. A creditor may also initiate bankruptcy proceedings against an individual in the event that both parties fail to reach an agreement on how the outstanding debt obligations will be settled.

Unemployment levels usually increase during times of economic uncertainty. A lot of people lose their jobs. Families/households sometimes are thus thrown into financial distress during such periods. The crisis may be so bad in some instances to the point that people are unable to provide their basic needs of food, shelter, clothing and basic health requirements.

Bankruptcy is obviously not a term that people love to mention. But it is a reality that we all must grapple with. Bankruptcy is all around us and at different levels of severity for different people. Personal bankruptcy can give rise to serious consequences for the individual and it is in the best interest of all to avoid it.

Consequences of Personal Bankruptcy

Personal bankruptcy can give rise to some of the following consequences:

1. Loss of personal assets.
2. Loss of reputation and credibility
3. Loss of employment
4. Poverty and Misery
5. Deprivation
6. Psychological trauma
7. Loss of faith in the political, social and economic systems
8. Increased tendency to engage in social vices
9. Desperation
10. Depression and ill health

It therefore means that the impact of bankruptcy occasioned by economic hardship on the individual may be classified according to the nature of the effect under the following categories.

1. Financial Impact
    I.   Loss of Employment
    II.   Loss of Personal Assets
    III.   Financial Poverty
    IV.   Lack of financial independence

2. Psychological Impact
    I.   Trauma
    II.   Loss of Self Confidence
    III.   Desperation
    IV.   Depression and Misery
    V.   Loss of feeling of self-worth
    VI.   Mental Ill Health
    VII.   Breeds Radical Tendencies

3. Social and Environmental Impact
    I.   Increase in social vices
    II.   Increase in financial crimes
    III.   Breakdown of moral and ethical values in society
    IV.   Compounds environmental problems with the economic destitution that it creates
    V.   Loss of faith in the political and economy systems of society

From the personal point of view, it is not necessary for an individual to wait until he/she cannot pay his/her debts before taking concrete steps to safeguard oneself from bankruptcy. Personal bankruptcy is one real and ever present danger to all who are involved in taking financial and economic decisions.

It is considered wise practice to always be on guard as the threat of bankruptcy is always lurking on the sidelines. For instance, an individual who earns a very high income and yet is imprudent in the management of financial resources always faces the threat of a sudden bankruptcy.

Any individual who is in any of the following circumstances may be bankrupt or facing the threat of imminent bankruptcy:

1. Someone whose income cannot support his mortgage payments.
2. Someone whose credit card debts for sundry purchases cannot be offset by regular income.
3. Someone who has lost his/her employment and hence major source of income.
4. Someone whose back-up savings has been wiped-out.
5. Someone who is struggling on a daily, weekly or monthly basis to provide for basic physiological needs.
6. Someone with outstanding debt payment obligations whose period of grace has passed.
7. Someone that is employed and yet unsure about his ability to meet future financial and economic obligations from the employment income.
8. Someone who lacks spending discipline.
9. Someone who spends all his/her income without making any savings or investments.
10. Someone who is unskilled and unwilling to learn and work.
11. Someone who is skilled and yet is unwilling to work.
12. Someone who does not have a future financial plan or a retirement plan in place.

It is thus obvious that from the personal or individual point of view the threat of bankruptcy is ever present, real and imminent. Unlike business and national bankruptcies that may occur over a period of time when the appropriate system of controls are not implemented, personal bankruptcy may occur in an instant once the principles guiding sound management of personal finances are violated.

The only control available to prevent personal bankruptcy comes from the individual himself. And the individual, being an emotional being may be at risk due to pressures from the immediate social and political environment.

Personal debts naturally increase the risk of personal bankruptcy as it gives the creditor the right to initiate bankruptcy proceedings in the event of a debt default. For the management of personal finances, the golden rule is to live within your means. That way the individual retains the right to declare whether he or she is bankrupt or not.

In periods of economic uncertainties such as in a recession or in a depression, the emotions tend to seize consumers and investors. Fear, anxiety, remorse and depression tend to take hold of people. The herd instinct appears to be high as consumers and investors tend to exhibit similar behavior traits. The markets dictate the pace of events even when chosen courses of herd actions as characterized by the market may appear questionable.

It is most likely that in periods of economic uncertainties, decisions by investors and consumers are driven more by emotional considerations rather than rational considerations. Such moments are characterized by panic, which also serves to heighten the general level of uncertainties. There is thus a serious flight of investment capital in addition to a sharp decline in consumer spending, particularly on luxury goods for most economies that are enmeshed in an economic crisis.

To thrive in a period of economic hardship, individuals must be armed with the right knowledge and skills required to take the proper decisions needed to overcome the economic challenges of each period. A combination of the right thought framework and actions consistently applied is required as a protective measure against personal bankruptcy at all times.

CHAPTER SIX

Business/Company Bankruptcy

Business failure often leads to bankruptcy. When a business or company is unable to meet its debts obligations to creditors and is unable to refinance its operations through injection of fresh capital or loans, the business is then headed for bankruptcy. Corporate bankruptcy proceedings involve legal actions. The legal action ensures the orderly resolution of credit obligations owed by a company, firm or business. Different countries have different provisions within their laws designed to accommodate the filing of bankruptcy by businesses.

CAUSES OF BUSINESS BANKRUPTCY

Basically the myriad causes that can lead to corporate bankruptcy can be categorized under two main headings:

1. External factors
2. Internal factors

External Factors

External factors are those that are outside the control of the business or company. Being outside the control of the business implies that the best the business can do is to anticipate undesirable changes in those factors and thus put in measures to mitigate their impact. External factors include:

1. A general decline in the economy
2. A sharp increase in the cost of inputs for the business
3. A serious drop in consumer demand
4. Increased competition
5. Declining industry performance
6. A drastic change in tax burden
7. Crystallization of heavy legal liabilities
8. New technological changes
9. Unfriendly/Hostile business environment
10. Natural Disasters/ Accidents/ Force majeure

Internal Factors

Internal factors are those within the control of the business internal stakeholders such as the board of directors, management team or even the employees. To a large extent, the company or business can determine the nature of these factors. Interestingly, experiences from large business failures of the past decades result more from factors that are within the control of the business than from those factors that are external to the business. Internal factors that may lead to business failure and thus business bankruptcy include the following:

1. Absence of good corporate governance practices
2. Management incompetence
3. Weak systems of internal control
4. Poor business planning
5. Financial mismanagement
6. Heavy debt burden
7. Poor liquidity management practices
8. Poor product portfolio
9. Unresolved labor disputes
10. Lack of proper attention to the requirement of the regulatory, legal and tax environments

It is important to note that once any of these factors is not properly put in check, it can create a chain reaction and the setting off of many other factors that combine to lead to a situation of financial difficulty.

For instance, a business with poor liquidity management practices does not pay good attention to its cash flow management. When this company defaults consistently in paying employees their wages as at when due, this could create a dispute between employees and the management team. If this liquidity problem is not nipped in the bud, future reoccurrence can create a culture of hostility between the employees and the management team. Staff morale, welfare and productivity are negatively impacted. The company is prone to sabotage from its employees.

Options for a Business facing Financial Difficulty

Financial challenge is part and parcel of everyday business life. Funds have to be sourced from various sources in order to be used for various business purposes. As businesses desire to be profitable, they must also pay attention to the way they manage cash flow.

Cash flow or the flow of cash into and out of the business is the life blood of any successful enterprise. Because of this, a very profitable business can experience serious liquidity problems if good attention is not paid to the management of its cash flow. If a company has good cash flow management practices, even while unprofitable, it can thrive in a gloomy economic climate until the general business environment improves to bring it back to profitability.

When a business is confronted with serious financial difficulties, it is left with any of the following three options:

Option 1:   Refinance
Option 2:   Default
Option 3:   File for Bankruptcy

Refinancing gives the company the opportunity to seek for additional funds in the form of capital or business loans to help it attend to its most pressing needs. For this option to be feasible, the business case for the business needs to be positive. The future prospects of the business must remain quite high and its plans must be achievable. Refinancing gives the business enterprise more time and opportunity to bounce back.

A debt default affects the company's credit rating and it could lead to litigations from creditors and other stakeholders. For the business debts that are secured, there is the risk of loss of those assets that have been provided as collateral. Where sensitive business assets have been provided as collateral for business loans, a debt repayment default has the potential to completely disrupt the operations of a business. It is as such understandable why this is usually the least considered option.

Filing a business bankruptcy enables a business to seek protection from litigation by the creditors. In the United States of America and other countries, bankruptcy proceedings may lead to any of the following:

1. Restructuring of the business
2. Liquidation of the business

A restructuring of the business could be carried out in order to keep it in business after settlement of its debts. When a business is liquidated, its assets are disposed off in order to settle its creditors. In the process, binding agreements that created debt obligations are prioritized and settled in an orderly manner. In the event of liquidation, a trustee is usually assigned for the business facing financial difficulties.

Businesses that choose the option of filing for bankruptcy in times of financial difficulties must note that their reputation will go down following this action. Their credit ratings will certainly drop and this might make it a bit more difficult to secure new loans in the event that they choose to remain in business.

Impact of Business Bankruptcy on the Individual, the Industry and the Economy

When a business is declared bankrupt, even if it does not go into liquidation, restructuring implies that its operations will shrink following the disposal of some assets belonging to the business.

Once the capacity shrinks, then layoffs become inevitable. Some employees are bound to be out of work creating a cycle of economic and social problems for individuals and households. An employee that has been thrown out of work in the event of a business restructuring faces financial, social and psychological problems. As a result of factors that are not of his own doing, suddenly this individual is unable to pay some of his bills. Mortgage debts(if any) remain one of the biggest financial burdens.

Where a business is liquidated as a result of bankruptcy, the entire workforce of the company is effectively thrown into the labor market. For some of the employees, this could mean starting all over again from the scratch. The misery is compounded when there are heavy third party debt obligations that were tied to the lost employment. In effect, this situation compels all the former employees of the company to practically restructure their lives again.

Individuals (particularly company employees) are amongst those who suffer untold hardship as a result of business bankruptcies. Being without a source of regular income creates serious psychological, social and economic problems for people and households. The ensuring financial deprivation leads to misery, depression and sometimes destitution.

In a highly integrated industry where businesses interact frequently, the failure of one business or company can precipitate failures for other related business and eventually lead to a collapse of the industry. However, the extent of business integration and dependence is the key factor that determines whether the failure of a single company or a collection of companies can lead to a collapse of the industry. Where businesses in an industry are highly integrated, interrelated and interdependent, such an industry may best be described as a fragile industry. A very good example is the banking and finance industry in most nations.

Due to the very fragile nature of the banking industry in many nations, the 2007/2008 global financial crisis led to a regime of significant government bailout of the banks in many nations. One major bank failure can threaten the entire financial industry and once the health of the financial industry is at risk, the entire economic system of a country is also at risk.

Types of Business Failure

From the practical point of view, business failures may take the form of any of the following two types:

1. The Sudden Failure or Sudden Death
2. The Gradual Failure of Phased Failure

The sudden failure gives no sign. It appears from nowhere and simply strikes. The speed is so sudden that it leaves no one with any room for preparation. Both internal and external factors can lead to the sudden death of a business. Unethical management practices that have been hidden from the public eye can lead to a sudden death scenario once the news breaks. The distinguishing element of this type of business failure is that the general public had no foreknowledge that such a business manifested symptoms that could lead to failure. Factors that lead to sudden death of businesses are usually major and impact heavily on the ability of the business to remain in operation such factors may include:

1. A major natural disaster such as a tsunami, earthquake, floods, firestorm etc
2. A major financial fraud
3. Radical changes in government rules for business
4. Outcome of a major litigation
5. Overnight collapse of the industry

The gradual type of business failure occurs over a period of time. Quite often, there are tell-tale signs that a particular business is slowly moving towards extinction.

Symptoms especially within the business point to the direction of difficulty, crisis and extinction. Well established businesses in matured industries usually exhibit a phased pattern of failure. The symptoms of poor performance occasioned by management incompetence in a rapidly evolving business environment are usually there as red flags. A defining element of this type of business failure is the symptom of poor performance. A history of poor performance resulting from management's inability to respond adequately to the challenges of the business environment leads to business decline and failure.

Figure 6: The Phases of Gradual Business Failure

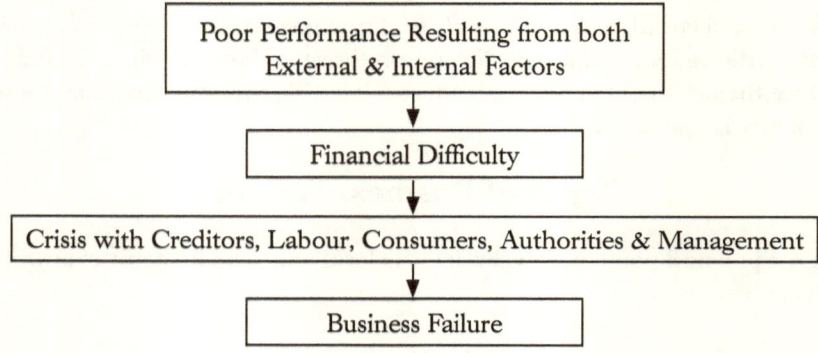

Some Recent Business Bankruptcies

ENRON CORPORATION – DECEMBER 2001

Enron's collapse is widely attributed to creative accounting practices that concealed the results of billions of dollars of bad businesses over the years. As at the time of filing for its bankruptcy in December 2001, Enron's was worth about $63.4 billion (Sixty Three Billion, Four Hundred Million US Dollars). This was the largest corporate bankruptcy in U.S history as at that time.

It is reported that stock holders lost over $11 billion (Eleven Billion US Dollars) in the crash of the market price of Enron's shares. The Enron scandal was revealed sometime in October 2001.

Apart from the bankruptcy of the Enron Corporation, the biggest audit failure of that time led to the dissolution of Arthur Andersen. It is reported that risky accounting practices were used to conceal the negative results of many transactions of the energy firm that had failed. The executives of Enron were found to have deliberately misled the Board and the Audit Committee on the contents of their financial reports. As auditors to Enron Corporation, Arthur Andersen was held to have failed in its responsibility of informing the shareholders on the true state of affairs of the Enron Corporation.

The Enron scandal threw up the following challenges for businesses, the accounting and audit professions:

1.   What is the role of ethics in business leadership?
2.   What are good corporate governance practices in a business?
3.   Reforms to handle creative accounting practices.
4.   Conflict of interests between auditors also acting as consultants to businesses.
5.   Off balance sheet items and financial reporting.
6.   The importance of avoiding complex business models.

WORLDCOM – JULY 2002

WorldCom's bankruptcy was precipitated by a major accounting fraud in which it is reported that the company's assets had been overestimated to the tune of $11 billion (Eleven Billion US Dollars). With about $107 billion dollars in assets, it was considered one of the largest long-distance telecommunications companies in the United States of America prior to bankruptcy.

The WorldCom scandal is a good example of how sharp accounting practices such as a fraud can lead to company failure. As a large telecommunications company that was doing well in the eyes of the public, the failure of WorldCom also raised issues of business honesty and integrity. The executives of WorldCom were determined to give the company a positive image.

WorldCom engaged in the process of acquiring a number to telecommunications companies. Large funds of monies moving in and out of the company were improperly monitored. To prove that the company was profitable, the figures were inflated to create an impression of good health. The WorldCom experience also reemphasized the need for the following:

1.   Financial accountability
2.   The role of the Board of Directors in corporate governance
3.   The importance of the independent audit function

Having experienced quick loss of profits in addition to the accounting frauds, WorldCom filed for bankruptcy in July 2002. At that time, it was the biggest bankruptcy filing in the United States. The accounting fraud at WorldCom was committed in different ways:

Firstly, interconnection expenses with other telecom service providers were underreported. Rather than expensing the interconnect charges, they were capitalized effectively reducing them.

Secondly, WorldCom also engaged in revenue inflation by posting unearned income into the accounts. The combination of cost underreporting and revenue inflation led to a crisis of confidence in the company's share when the news of the fraud broke.

LEHMAN BROTHERS – SEPTEMBER 2008

The collapse of the financial giant; Lehman Brothers in September 2008 is considered the most complex case of corporate bankruptcy in the world. A culture of high risk business initiatives coupled with poor financial accountability led to company failure.

With over $600 billion (Six Hundred Billion US Dollars) in assets, this bankruptcy is the largest one in US history. The collapse of Lehman Brothers is a fall-out of the 2007/2008 global financial crisis. Lehman Brothers had borrowed significantly and invested in the housing industry.

Faced with significant losses in the subprime mortgage sector in 2008, the company stock values fell. With an increasing credit squeeze, the company planned to reduce its staff strength.

Continuing fall in the stock values of Lehman Brothers further eroded investor confidence. Even with further concerns about the safety and security of the bank, plans were not announced by the government on any mode of assistance for the bank as at 9th September 2008.

When on 15th September 2008 Lehman Brothers filed for bankruptcy, it had $639 billion (Six Hundred and Thirty Nine Billion Dollars) in assets and $619 (Six Hundred and Nineteen Dollars) in debt. This was the single largest bankruptcy filing in US history as at 2008.

With a network of offices across many countries of the world and with over 25,000 (Twenty Five Thousand) staff strength, this bankruptcy is one of the largest in scale in modern history. As the fourth largest investment bank in the United States, the multiplier effect of the Lehman Brothers' collapse significantly contributed to the worsening of the global financial crisis.

Significant losses were recorded by investors in stock markets across the globe as market confidence was seriously affected by this bankruptcy. The failure of Lehman Brothers remains a very good test case for the following:

1. How the subprime mortgage crisis in the United States led to the collapse of a major financial institution?
2. How the failure of one major financial institution can lead to an industry crisis?
3. How the financial crisis of one nation affects the financial markets of other nations?

CHAPTER SEVEN

National Bankruptcy

When the government of a nation is unable to settle its outstanding debt obligations to creditors as at when due, it is faced with the scenario of a national bankruptcy. Governments are institutions that acquire assets and incur liabilities. Governments also have responsibilities to many of its stakeholders such as its citizens, creditors, trading partners and multilateral organizations.

The impact of a national bankruptcy can lead to drastic and radical changes within the economic and political structure of society. Individuals, businesses, industries and other national economies are impacted. History has shown that a national bankruptcy can lead to a complete collapse of the government in power.

As a sovereign entity, a nation has responsibility to protect its independence and territorial integrity. This is in addition to providing the basic social services that are necessary to ensure the smooth functioning of a modern state. Apart from the disruption of the economic life of the state, a national bankruptcy can ultimately lead to the decline of a state and eventually a failed state.

History of National Bankruptcies

National bankruptcies are not new to the modern world. But the looming European sovereign debt crisis presents serious concerns in terms of its complexity and the scope of its likely impact on the overall global economy. The following are some historical examples of national bankruptcies:

1. In 1557, Spain became the first sovereign state in history to declare bankruptcy. Spain had defaulted on its loan payments on so many occasions prior to this. The increasing cost of providing military services was responsible for this debt default scenario. The 1557 declaration of bankruptcy was followed up by three (3) other bankruptcy declarations in 1560, 1575 and 1596.
2. Denmark also declared bankruptcy in 1813.
3. Germany: In the 1920's.
4. The Executive Order 6102 of the United States of America which led to the confiscation of gold in private hands in 1933 is considered a declaration of national bankruptcy.
5. Great Britain: In the 1940's as a result of the 2nd World War.
6. The repudiation of the dollar gold convertibility by the United States of America in 1971 is also considered a declaration of national bankruptcy.
7. The Russian financial crisis of 1998 is considered a declaration of national bankruptcy in 1998.
8. Argentina: Between the years 1999-2002.
9. Zimbabwe: The ongoing hyperinflation and currency crisis of Zimbabwe.
10. Iceland: The 2008 Global Financial Crisis.

Causes of National Bankruptcies

Because the economic structures of countries differ. The nature of this structure creates the causes of national bankruptcy. Some of the common causes include:

1. Too much sovereign debt
2. Significant loss of government revenue from taxation
3. Dwindling revenue from a national resource that has become a major income earner for the national government such as solid minerals, crude oil and gas
4. High government fiscal deficits
5. Mismanagement of financial resources
6. Domestic financial crisis
7. Natural disasters
8. War
9. Spread of international economic crisis
10. Incompetent political & economic leadership

Those Impacted by National bankruptcies

1. The Individual
2. The Business and Industry
3. The Government
4. The Creditors of the State (Domestic and International)
5. The Country's International Trading Partners.

Figure 6: The Ensuing Crisis Pattern following a National Bankruptcy

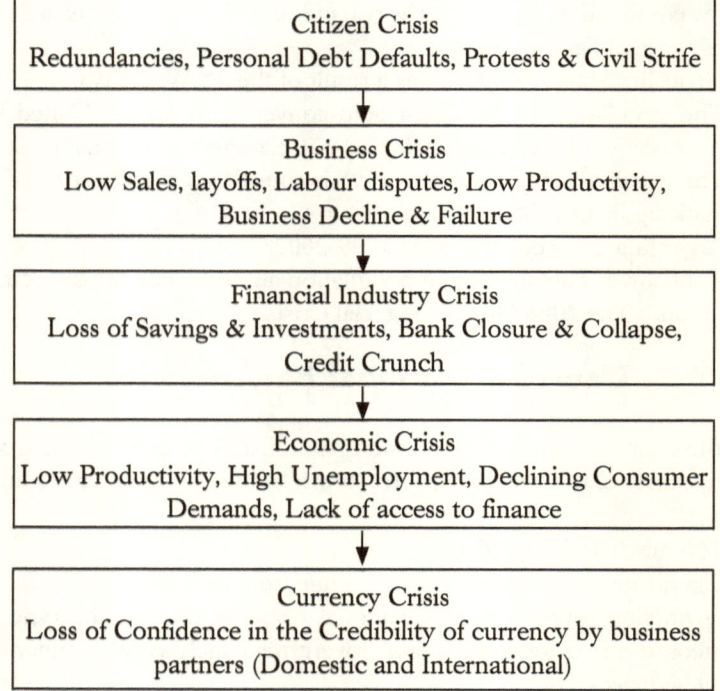

Just the way a national bankruptcy can lead to a sequence of crisis in different areas of the given economic environment, factors in that economic environment can also precipitate the onset of national bankruptcy. There appears to be a two-way cause and effect relationship between these factors and national bankruptcy.

Figure 8: The Cause Effect Relationship

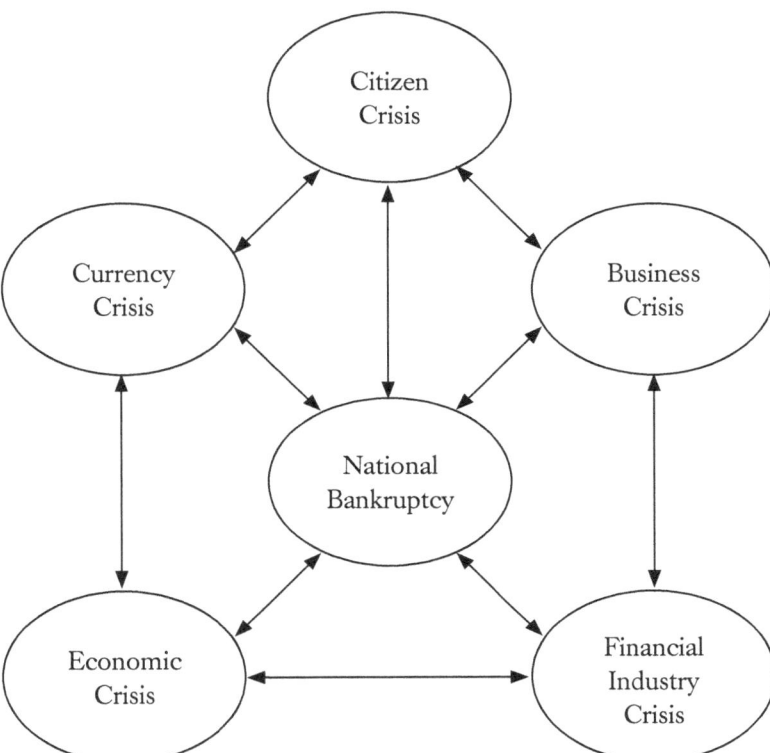

A national bankruptcy may lead to a change in political leadership of the government. The sentiment of nationalism is usually strongest in nations facing the challenges of an economic crisis. The political crisis as such may occur at any stage of these events. A change in government does not imply that the economic problems no longer exist. It may simply signify a change in the economic policy thrust of a new political leadership.

The prospects of the looming European sovereign debt crisis and its possible ripple effects across the world has created deep anxieties amongst individuals, businesses and nations in all parts of the globe. Should a few number of euro zone countries default on their sovereign debt repayments, the crisis could spread to the United States of America. With a fragile financial system in the US, it is inconceivable how much damage could be done to asset values in stock exchanges across the globe. The Euro currency and the entire economy of the euro zone are certainly at risk from the possible collapse of the European financial system.

Suffice it to state than in the event of a national bankruptcy, the credibility of the political leadership is always called to question. Unlike in a business failure where it is relatively easy to make a change in business leadership the same is not the case for the political leadership of a state or nation.

While a national bankruptcy may lead to a change in political leadership, the legitimacy of this process of change in political leadership is an issue of grave concern.

PART THREE

CRAFTING THE
ECONOMIC SURVIVAL PLAN

CHAPTER EIGHT

Crafting a Survival Plan: The Individual

The individual is the human organ who bears the brunt of economic uncertainties. He feels the direct pain of the downturn in the general economy. Either as an employee, employer, business manager or political leader, the incidence of an economic crisis might compel the individual to go through a range of the following emotions and feelings:

1. Disappointment
2. Anger
3. Frustration
4. Despair
5. Hopelessness
6. Fear
7. Confusion
8. Dejection
9. Irritation
10. Provocation
11. Foolishness
12. Faithlessness in leadership

An individual who experiences a range of the above emotions is bound to be on the downside psychologically. Loss of employment and loss of income occasioned by an economic crisis erodes the personal confidence of people in society. This scenario can set off a chain of events that may eventually lead to drastic change in the political and economic structure of society.

In crafting an economic survival plan for the individual, the following five scenarios of the individual have been considered:

1. Scenario 1:   An individual that is employed, but at the risk of layoff.
2. Scenario 2:   An individual that is out of work in a depressed economy.
3. Scenario 3:   An individual whose reduced present income can no longer support his debt (mortgage) obligations.
4. Scenario 4:   An individual who has lost significant values of stock investments.
5. Scenario 5:   An individual who lacks financial discipline even before the outset of the economic crisis.

Scenario 1:   Employed But at the Risk of a Layoff

The following 5-step tips are recommended:

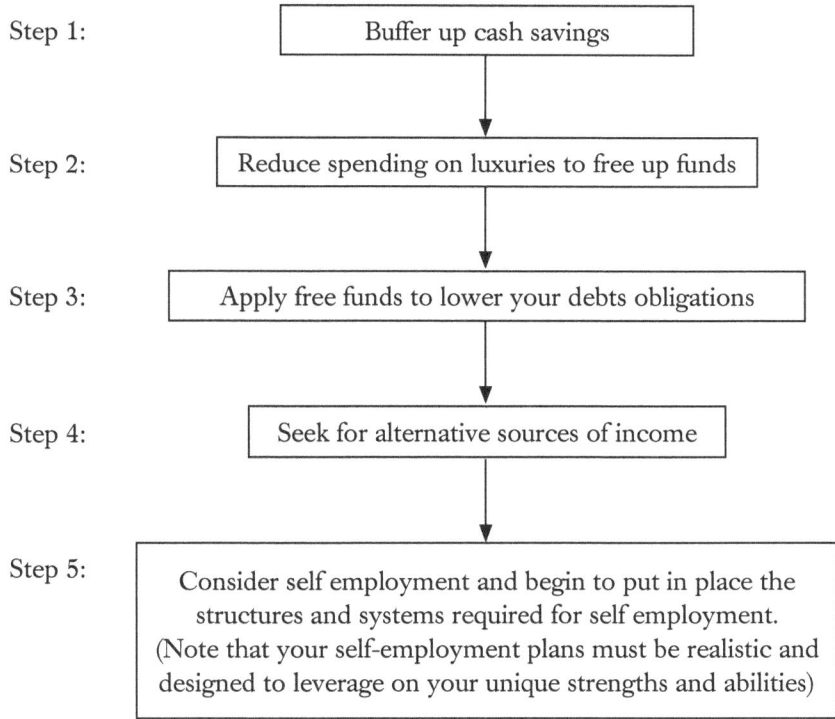

Step 1:   Buffer up cash savings

Step 2:   Reduce spending on luxuries to free up funds

Step 3:   Apply free funds to lower your debts obligations

Step 4:   Seek for alternative sources of income

Step 5:   Consider self employment and begin to put in place the structures and systems required for self employment. (Note that your self-employment plans must be realistic and designed to leverage on your unique strengths and abilities)

Scenario 2: Out of Work in a Depressed Economy

The following 5-step tips are also recommended:

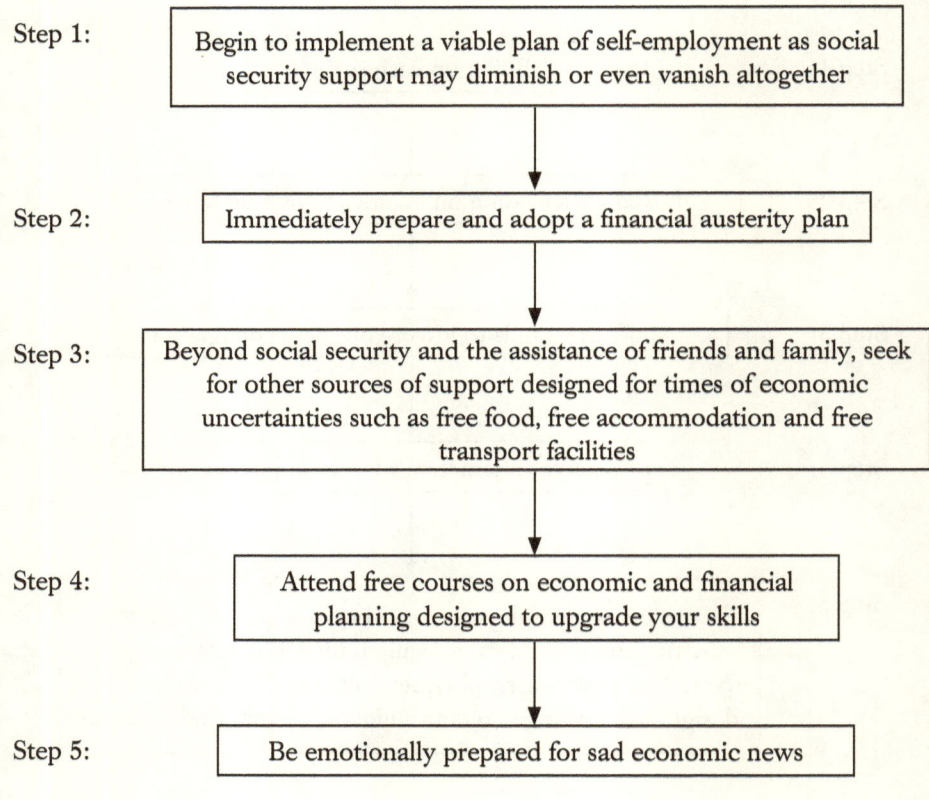

Step 1:   Begin to implement a viable plan of self-employment as social security support may diminish or even vanish altogether

Step 2:   Immediately prepare and adopt a financial austerity plan

Step 3:   Beyond social security and the assistance of friends and family, seek for other sources of support designed for times of economic uncertainties such as free food, free accommodation and free transport facilities

Step 4:   Attend free courses on economic and financial planning designed to upgrade your skills

Step 5:   Be emotionally prepared for sad economic news

Scenario 3: Income no longer able to support payment of debts and mortgages

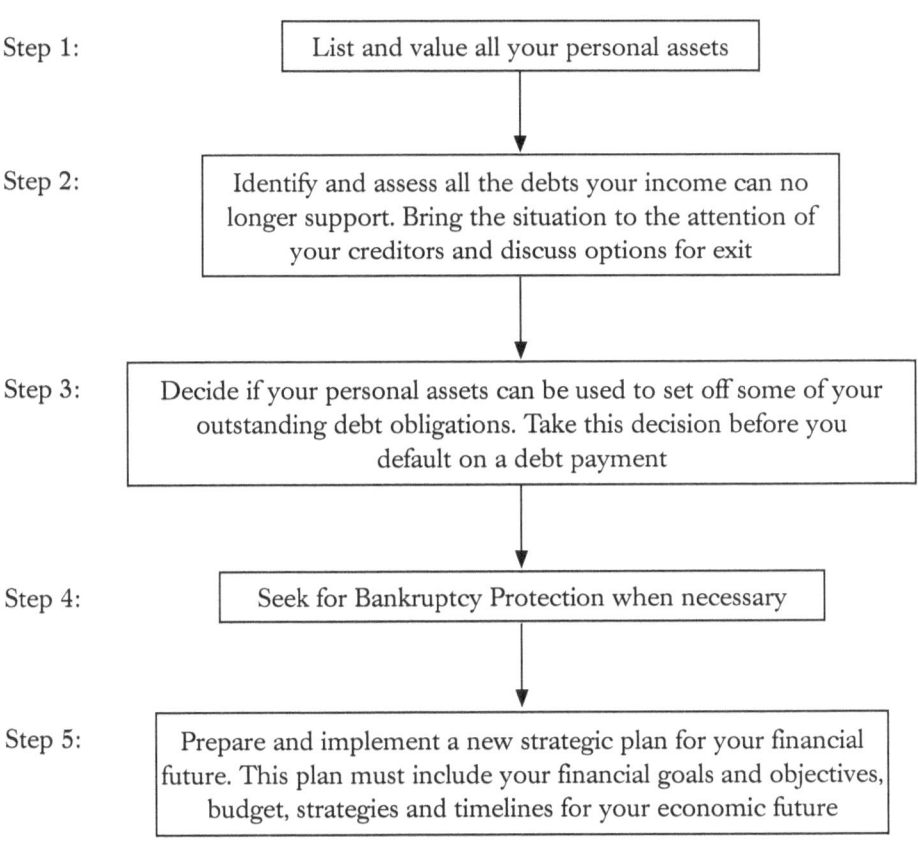

Step 1:   List and value all your personal assets

Step 2:   Identify and assess all the debts your income can no longer support. Bring the situation to the attention of your creditors and discuss options for exit

Step 3:   Decide if your personal assets can be used to set off some of your outstanding debt obligations. Take this decision before you default on a debt payment

Step 4:   Seek for Bankruptcy Protection when necessary

Step 5:   Prepare and implement a new strategic plan for your financial future. This plan must include your financial goals and objectives, budget, strategies and timelines for your economic future

Scenario 4: Loss of significant value of stock investments

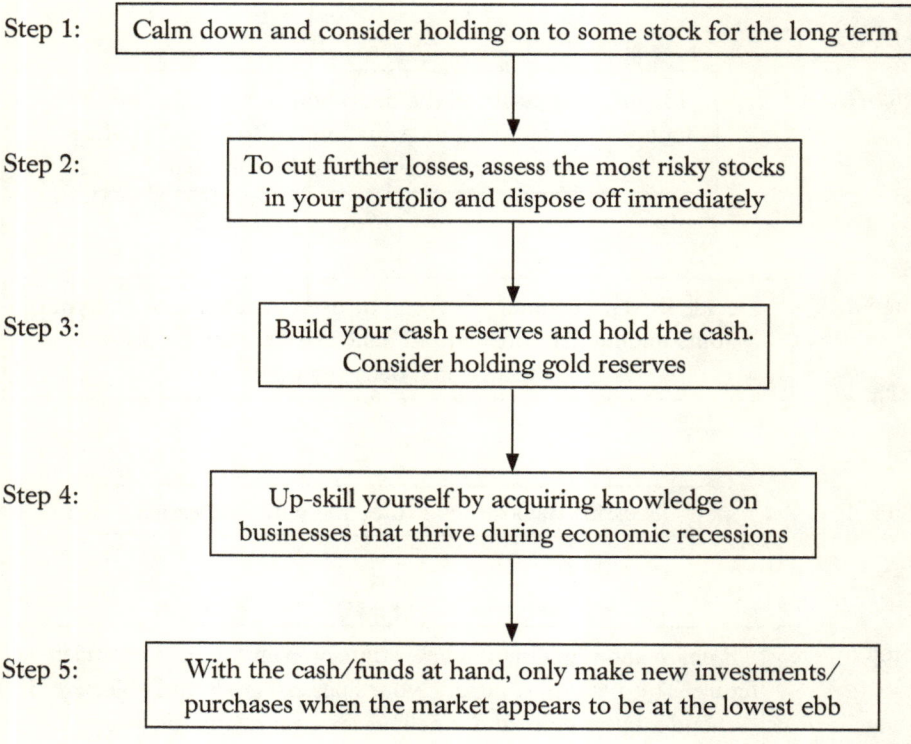

Step 1: Calm down and consider holding on to some stock for the long term

Step 2: To cut further losses, assess the most risky stocks in your portfolio and dispose off immediately

Step 3: Build your cash reserves and hold the cash. Consider holding gold reserves

Step 4: Up-skill yourself by acquiring knowledge on businesses that thrive during economic recessions

Step 5: With the cash/funds at hand, only make new investments/ purchases when the market appears to be at the lowest ebb

Scenario 5: Lack of financial discipline

An individual who lacks financial discipline already faces a constant threat of personal bankruptcy with all its attendant consequences. However, economic depression presents this individual with a clean opportunity for positive change or personal destruction. It could create a good opportunity for deep reflection or it could worsen that already poor attitude to the management of finances. For this individual, the following 5 step tips are apt:

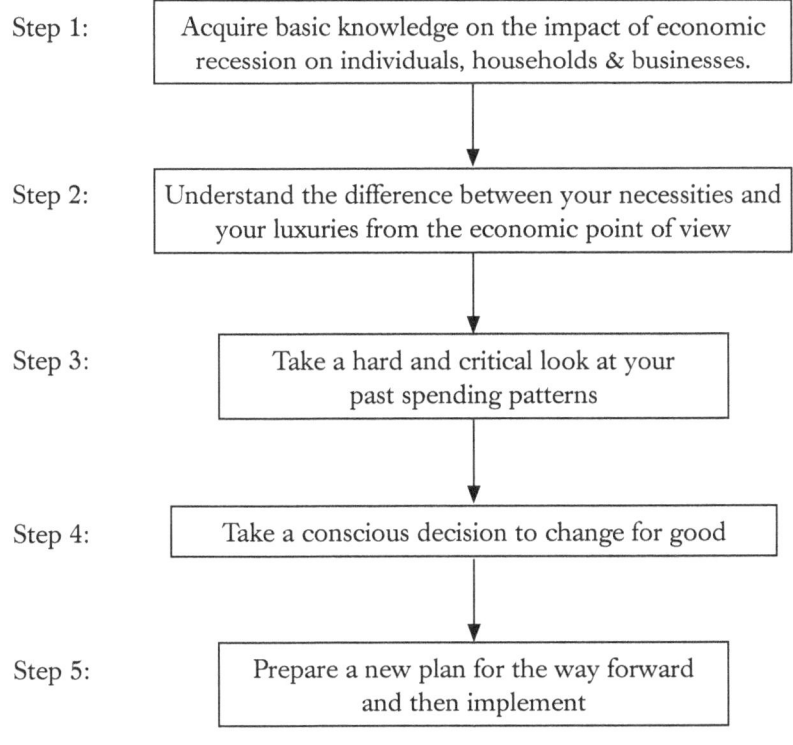

Step 1:   Acquire basic knowledge on the impact of economic recession on individuals, households & businesses.

Step 2:   Understand the difference between your necessities and your luxuries from the economic point of view

Step 3:   Take a hard and critical look at your past spending patterns

Step 4:   Take a conscious decision to change for good

Step 5:   Prepare a new plan for the way forward and then implement

CHAPTER NINE

Crafting a Survival Plan—The Business

An economic recession/depression almost always affects the financial industry. A financial crisis is thus a symptom of the general economic crisis occasioned by bank failures and business failures.

When a particular business entity is central to the economy of a nation, a failure of that business can lead to a financial crisis in the banking industry. Likewise, the failure of a major financial institution can lead to the collapse of the financial industry and by extension other businesses and industries that are highly integrated with the financial industry.

Because companies/firms in the financial industry provide a unique nature of services, their focal points of interest in a depressed economy may be slightly different from that of firms in other sectors of the economy.

For the purposes of crafting an economic survival plan for businesses (which includes banks and other businesses in the financial industry), the following general classifications are made:

1. Scenario 1:   Businesses in the financial industry
2. Scenario 1:   Businesses in the non-financial industries

Scenario 1: Business in the Financial Industry

Financial businesses are principally concerned about the following factors in periods of economic uncertainties:

1. Their exposures to other financial institutions within the industry (domestic and international).
2. Their exposure to key economic drivers (business and industries) of the economy.
3. Their exposures to drastic changes in government policy and requirements.

Because of the above reasons the following 5-step tips are recommended for businesses in the financial industry during periods of economic downturns:

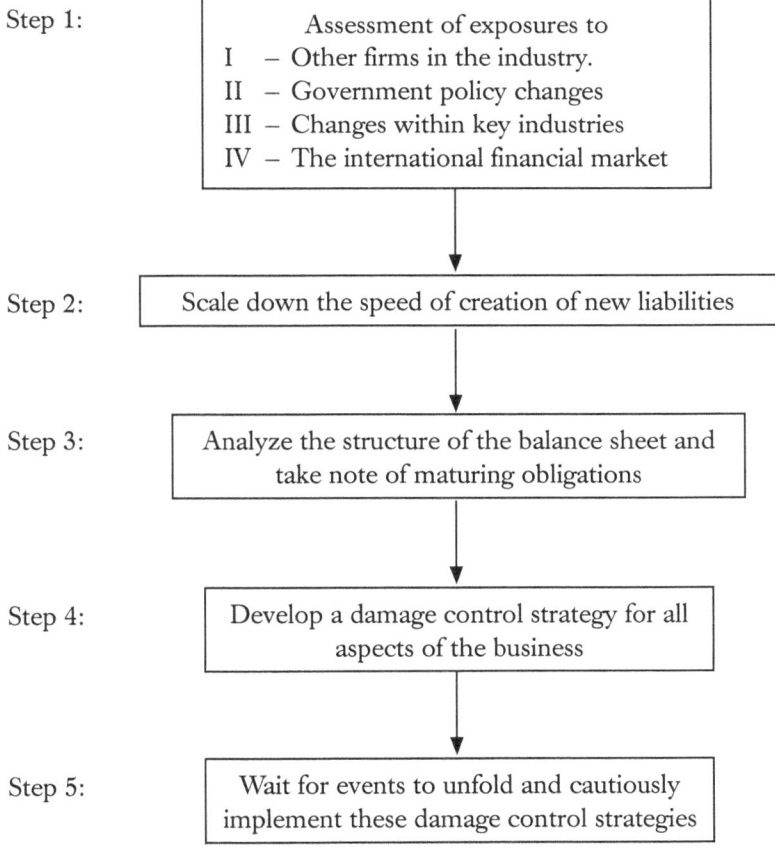

Step 1:

Assessment of exposures to
I   – Other firms in the industry.
II – Government policy changes
III – Changes within key industries
IV – The international financial market

Step 2:

Scale down the speed of creation of new liabilities

Step 3:

Analyze the structure of the balance sheet and take note of maturing obligations

Step 4:

Develop a damage control strategy for all aspects of the business

Step 5:

Wait for events to unfold and cautiously implement these damage control strategies

Scenario 2: Businesses in the Non-Financial Industries

A non-financial business is typically concerned about the following during periods of economic uncertainty:

1. Whether the business is in a declining industry?
2. The level of dependence and this exposure of the business to the financial industry.
3. Whether the business in endowed with the appropriate mix of leadership, employees, systems and procedures that will enable it thrive in difficult times.
4. The level of dependence of the business on international trade with other countries.
5. The future financial viability of the business in light of current economic realities.

For the above scenario, the following 5-step tips are recommended:

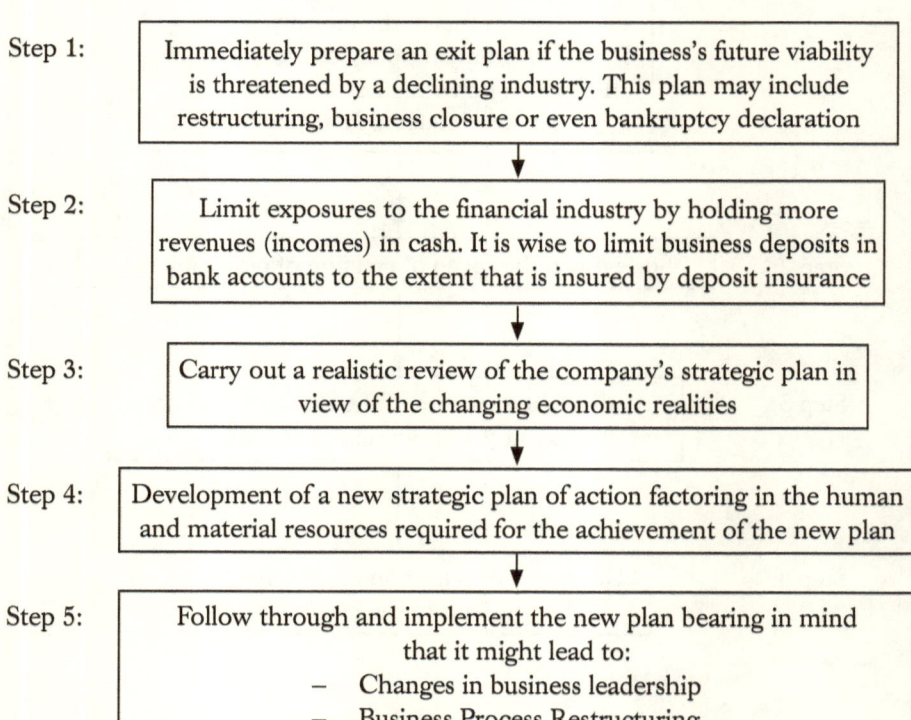

Step 1:
Immediately prepare an exit plan if the business's future viability is threatened by a declining industry. This plan may include restructuring, business closure or even bankruptcy declaration

Step 2:
Limit exposures to the financial industry by holding more revenues (incomes) in cash. It is wise to limit business deposits in bank accounts to the extent that is insured by deposit insurance

Step 3:
Carry out a realistic review of the company's strategic plan in view of the changing economic realities

Step 4:
Development of a new strategic plan of action factoring in the human and material resources required for the achievement of the new plan

Step 5:
Follow through and implement the new plan bearing in mind that it might lead to:
- Changes in business leadership
- Business Process Restructuring
- Business Changes
- Business Contraction etc.

CHAPTER TEN

Crafting a Survival Plan—The Nation

The twenty first (21st) Century appears to have presented a unique challenge to modern economic management. Rapid industrialization at the beginning of the twentieth (20th) century led to a massive increase in the production of goods and services. This production continued to increase to the point whereby global demand was not strong enough to consume the produced output. This low demand for products in addition to other factors contributed to the economic recession and subsequently depression of the 1930's.

Globalization appears to contain both positive and negative elements. It is clear that the world is indeed a global village where success and failure can easily cross national boundaries. Although, this is not the first time the world has experienced national bankruptcies, what is about to hit the global community with respect to the European sovereign debt crisis is unprecedented in history. Palpable fear appears to have gripped the top economic manages of all nations with particular reference to the unpredictable globalization of the sovereign debt crisis.

According to the International Monetary Fund, there appears to be a two-speed recovery pattern from the 2007/2008 global financial crisis. The developed economies appear to exhibit a lower GDP growth rate while the emerging and developing countries tend to reveal a higher annual GDP growth rate.

It has been generally observed that the two categorization of nation states have the following economic features:

1. Developed Economies – Low GDP Growth, Low Inflation Rate
2. Emerging and Developing Economies – Higher GDP Growth Rate, Higher Inflation Rate

With a national bankruptcy, economic indicators point in a downward trend as productivity, international trade and consumer demand spiral downwards. In terms of the impact of a national bankruptcy on the domestic economy, the effect is similar for most nations. However, because the economic structures of nation states are different, the severity of the crisis will be different.

In view of the above, it is considered appropriate to recommend economic survival tips for the 2 different broad categories of nations in the world economy.

Scenario 1:   The Developed Economies

Generally in 2011, the developed economies currently have the following features:

*   High levels of industrialization.
*   High GDP to Debt Ratios
*   Low GDP Growth Rate
*   Low Inflation
*   Fragile Banking Systems
*   High Levels of Specialization
*   High Levels of Government Fiscal deficits.
*   Free market economies
*   High level of integration with other developed economies.
*   High levels of integration with the international financial markets due to participation in the sovereign bonds market.

The above general features of developed economies present serious challenges for economic management

The following 5-step tips are thus recommended:

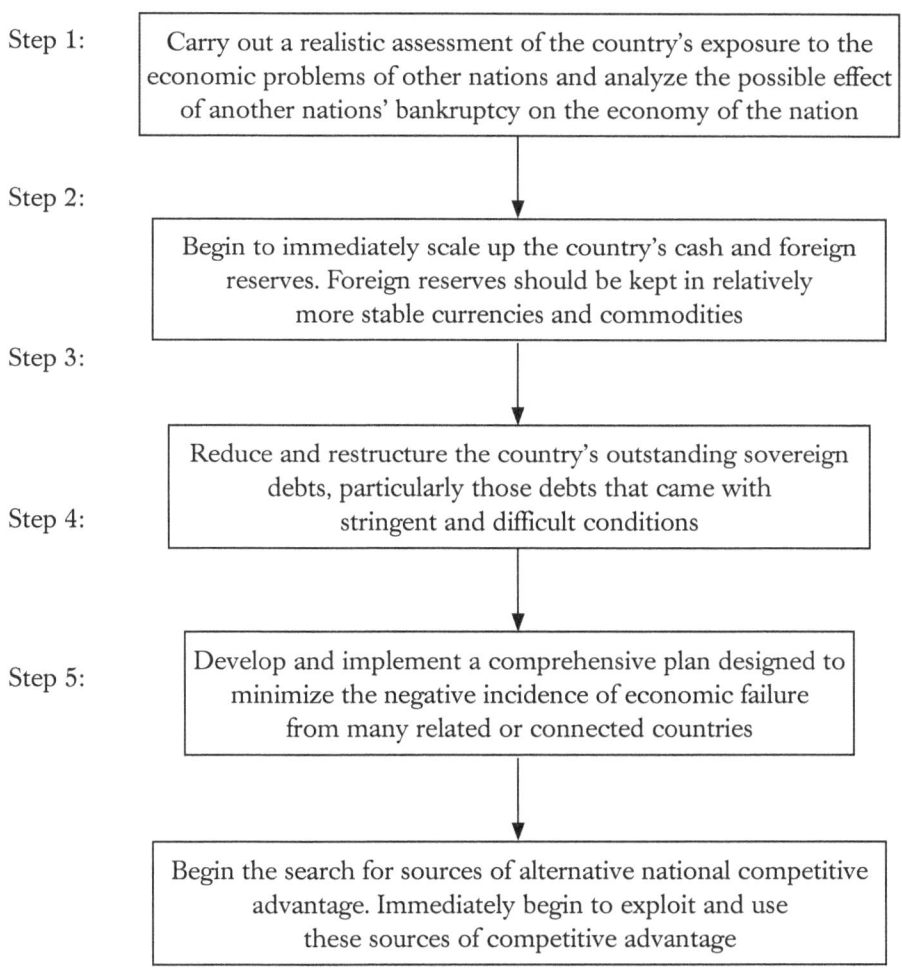

Step 1:

Carry out a realistic assessment of the country's exposure to the economic problems of other nations and analyze the possible effect of another nations' bankruptcy on the economy of the nation

Step 2:

Begin to immediately scale up the country's cash and foreign reserves. Foreign reserves should be kept in relatively more stable currencies and commodities

Step 3:

Reduce and restructure the country's outstanding sovereign debts, particularly those debts that came with stringent and difficult conditions

Step 4:

Develop and implement a comprehensive plan designed to minimize the negative incidence of economic failure from many related or connected countries

Step 5:

Begin the search for sources of alternative national competitive advantage. Immediately begin to exploit and use these sources of competitive advantage

Scenario 2: The Emerging and Developing Economies

Step 1:

> Carry out a detailed assessment of the country's exposure
> to the following factors:
> I   – The European nations at the risk of sovereign debt default
> II – The possibility of an economic crisis erupting in the USA
>   as a result of fiscal stimulus and a fragile financial system
> III - The possibility of an economic crisis in major trading nations

Step 2:

> Carry out a downward review of the following
> economic indicators:
> I - Foreign Direct Investment, particularly from nations
>   adjudged to be at risk of default
> II - The volume of international trade with all nations.
> III- GDP per capita

Step 3:

> Plan and implement an economic policy
> of fiscal consolidation by focusing of
> increasing national revenue and plugging
> all areas of wasteful expenditure

Step 4:

> Aggressively build the country's cash and foreign reserves.
> The foreign reserves could be maintained in stronger and
> relatively stable international currencies and commodities.

Step 5:

> Adopt an attitude of caution and conservatism in the
> further acquisition of sovereign debt and prudently
> manage the available liquid resources

Generally, the following tips are offered for all countries:

1. Beware of excess liquidity and liquidity squeeze.
2. Do not place too much reliance on the free market in resolving fundamental economic problems.
3. For industrializing nations, invest heavily in economic infrastructure as a way of taking care of the needs of the future.
4. For the industrialized nations, beware of the productivity shock.
5. Develop and adapt economic plans/models to suit the unique circumstances of the country.

CONCLUSION

Economic hardship caused by business, personal or national bankruptcy impacts on the health of individuals who are connected to the business or the economic system. Evidence has shown that the mental health of many is affected by the experiences of hunger, homelessness, physical sickness and economic destitution.

Presently, the following factors have continued to fuel global economic uncertainty at a tempo that is unprecedented:

1. The European Sovereign Debt Crisis
2. The US Debt Ceiling Debacle
3. Declining Economic Growth forecasts of developing countries.
4. Dampened IMF Economic Outlook for the entire globe.
5. Downgraded sovereign debt ratings of many countries by rating agencies.
6. Increasing fiscal deficit patterns in many developed economies.
7. Slow response of the political leadership to the challenges of economic management.
8. Increasing fears of economic downturn in Japan, India, China and other key Asian economies.

All these factors and many more tend to heighten the anxiety levels for individuals. People become highly sensitive and go through a wide range of emotions which includes:

- Anger
- Shock
- Disappointment
- Fear
- Emotional Depression

These emotions could lead to restlessness, lack of sleep and consistent worrying. When the mental stress reaches unbearable limits, some people even unfortunately consider suicide.

With the looming European sovereign debt crisis, the world economy has indeed entered a new dangerous phase. There is no doubt that a national bankruptcy in Europe can precipitate a major economic depression on a global scale. Although efforts by the European Union, the European Central Bank and the International Monetary Fund are in top gear to prevent such a crisis, many analysts are of the view that such efforts are mere window dressings to provide short-term financial life line support.

It is argued that unless fundamental shifts are made by addressing the root causes of the crisis rather than its symptoms. It is only a question of time before the crisis leads to a much bigger global economic and political crisis.

From my observation, it seems as though the world economy has not fully dealt with the 2007/2008 global financial crisis. If the 2011 sovereign debt crisis has its roots in the 2007/2008 global financial crisis, it therefore means that a more strategic and responsible approach is required for the global economy to emerge from the current gloomy prospects of the world economy.

With the above analogy, I join the call for the development of a long-term global economic strategy that is required for the global community to emerge from the looming danger. With the current trend in the globalization of economic success and failure, the world has indeed become a truly global village.

The present economic situation has proven one key point, that the world is interconnected and interdependent. Hence no real economic success is sustainable unless it promotes and guarantees the general good of all. The globalization of failure is indeed one of the earliest lessons of the twenty-first century.

NOTES

1. Allen, Robert G. Multiple Streams of Income: *How to Generate a Lifetime of Unlimited Wealth*. New Jersey: John Wiley & Sons, Inc, 2005.
2. Covey, Stephen R. *The 7 Habits of Highly Effective People*. New York: Simon and Schuster, 1998.
3. Hill, Napoleon. *Napoleon Hill's Keys to Success: the 17 Principles of Personal Achievement*. New York. Dutton. 1994.
4. Greene, Robert and Joost Elffers. *The 48 Laws of Power*. New York: Viking, 1998.
5. IMF World Economic Outlook (WEO) Update – Global Recovery Advances but Remains Uneven. *www.imf.org*. International Monetary Fund, January 2011.
6. IMF World Economic Outlook (WEO) – Tensions from the Two-Speed Recovery: Unemployment, Commodities, and Capital Flows. *www.imf.org*. International Monetary Fund, April 2011.
7. IMF World Economic Outlook (WEO) – Slowing Growth, Rising Risks. *www.imf.org*. International Monetary Fund, September 2011.
8. Irwin, Tim. *Run with the Bulls without Getting Trampled*. Nashville: Thomas Nelson, Inc. 2006.
9. Lakein, Alan. *How to Get Control of your Time and Your Life*. New American Library, 1996.
10. Maxwell, John C. *The 21 Irrefutable Laws of Leadership: Follow them and People will Follow You*. Nashville: Thomas Edison Publishers, 1998.
11. Noonan, David. *Aesop and the CEO: Powerful Business Insights from Aesop's Ancient Fables*. Nashville: Thomas Nelson Inc., 2005.
12. Orlowski, Lucjan T. Stages of the 2007/2008 Global Financial Crisis: Is there a wandering asset price bubble? A discussion paper. www.economics-ejournal.org, 2008.
13. Publication on *www.wikipedia.org*. National Bankruptcy. Wikipedia, the free encyclopedia, 2011.
14. Robbins, Anthony. *Awaken the Giant Within: How to take Immediate Control of your Mental, Emotional, Physical and Financial Destiny!* New York: Simon and Schuster New York, 1991.
15. Tracy, Brian. *Maximum Achievement: Strategies and Skills That Will Unlock Your Hidden Powers to Succeed*. Benin City: Beulahland Publications, 1993.
16. Trump, Donald. *The Art of the Deal*. New York: Random House, 1988.

Some Publications of the Author

Book

1. Mastering the Art of Managing Money

Some Economics and Finance Related Articles

1. The North Atlantic Debt Crisis: Lessons for Emerging and Developing Countries
2. Liquidity versus Profitability: The Dilemma of the Finance Manager
3. The Global Economic Crisis and the Challenge of Reforming Banking and Finance Practice.
4. The Icarus Paradox: Why some Nigerian Banks Failed
5. Nigeria's Sovereign Wealth Fund: Prospects and Tips for Getting it Right
6. Potentials of the Nigerian Sovereign Wealth Fund
7. Nigeria's Sovereign Wealth Fund: Avoiding the Pitfalls of Implementation
8. The IMF Article IV Consultation Report on Nigeria: Analysis and Implication
9. The Need for a Common Financial Accounting and Financial Reporting Framework for Nigerian Banks
10. Beyond the CAMELS Rating: A Model for Predicting Bank Failures in Nigeria

About the Author

Mr. Shafii Ndanusa *is a chartered accountant with memberships of the Association of Chartered Certified Accountants (ACCA, United Kingdom) and the Institute of Chartered Accountants of Nigeria (ACA; ICAN Nigeria). He holds the Master Financial Professional (MFP) charter of the American Academy of Financial Management (AAFM, USA) and is also designated as a Fellow of the American Academy of Financial Management (FAAFM, USA).*

Mr. Ndanusa *received his Bachelor of Science degree in Accounting from the University of Abuja, Nigeria and a Master of Business Administration degree from the Ahmadu Bello University Zaria, Nigeria. He is an acknowledged expert in enterprise financial management, wealth management, strategy development, business/economic research, statistical analysis and treasury management.*

Mr. Ndanusa *has carried out postgraduate research in the area of business bankruptcy prediction using financial ratio analysis for firms in the Nigerian oil industry. He has also carried out extensive professional research by modeling the bank failure characteristics of banks in the Nigerian financial system. He is a regular contributor to public debates on banking, economics and finance matters that are particularly relevant to Nigeria and other emerging/developing countries.*

He currently has over fifteen years of work experience cutting across a wide range of corporate finance and administration functions. He has authored over fifteen (15) professional papers that have been widely published. He is the author of the book titled, **Mastering the Art of Managing Money.**

Mr. Ndanusa *is currently a member of the Editorial Board of Advisors for the* **Financial Nigeria** *monthly journal, a leading monthly professional journal that focuses on contemporary economic development issues around the world and in particular, sub-Saharan Africa.*

His areas of general research interest include public finance policy/practice, financial management practice, banking, economic policy/strategy, wealth/asset management, business strategy and enterprise resource management. His hobbies include reading, writing and coaching. He lives in Abuja, Nigeria.